The Aquar

ERRATUM

When calculating your Ascendant on page 71,
please ignore the line which states:

2. Add 212 to this. New total is: ....

Bernard Fitzwalter has been interested in astrology since he was about six, when he played King Herod's astrologer in his primary school nativity play. For the past six years he has been teaching astrology for the Marylebone-Paddington Institute, and for seven years he has had a regular column in OVER 21 magazine. In 1984 he appeared in the first series of Anglia Television's *Zodiac Game*, which prompted the *Daily Mirror* to say that he was 'enough to give astrology a good name'.

AQUARIAN SUN SIGN GUIDES

CANCER

21 JUNE ~ 22 JULY

Bernard Fitzwalter

Cover illustration by Steinar Lund
Cover typography by Steven Lee

THE AQUARIAN PRESS
Wellingborough, Northamptonshire

First published 1987

British Library Cataloguing in Publication Data

Fitzwalter, Bernard
Cancer.—(The Aquarian sun sign guides)
1. Zodiac
I. Title
133.5'2   BF1726

ISBN 0-85030-585-3

*The Aquarian Press is part of the
Thorsons Publishing Group*

Printed and bound in Great Britain

Contents

PART 4: CANCER TRIVIA

Introduction

This book has been written to help you find out a little about astrology and a lot about yourself. It explains, for the first time, the motives and aims that guide your actions and make you do things the way you do; what it does not do is give you a list of 'typical Cancer' things to see if you recognize any of them. You are not likely to be typical anything: you are unique. What you *do* have in common with others who have birthdays at about the same time as you is a way of using your energy, a way of thinking, a set of motives and beliefs which seem to make sense to you, and which other people, those of the other eleven signs, obviously do not have. This book shows you those motives and beliefs, and shows you how they fit in with those of the other eleven signs. The zodiac is like a jigsaw: all the pieces have to be there for the whole picture to emerge.

This book also sets out to answer some very simple questions which are often asked but seldom answered. Questions like 'Why does the zodiac have twelve signs?' and 'What does being a Cancer actually mean?' as well as 'Why are Cancerians supposed to be compassionate? Why can't they be heartless instead? and why don't all the people of the same star sign look the same?'

The reason that these questions are seldom answered is because all too many astrologers don't know the rudiments of astrological theory, and what they do know they don't tell, because they think it is too difficult for the man in the street to understand. This is obvious nonsense: astrology was devised for and by people who did not normally read or write as much as we do, nor did they all have PhDs or the equivalent. The man in the street is quite capable of understanding anything provided that it is shown simply and clearly, from first principles upwards, and provided he has sufficient interest. Buying this book is evidence enough of your interest, and I hope that the explanations are simple enough and clear enough for you. If they are not, it is my fault, and not that of astrology.

How to Use this Book

The book is in four parts. It is best to read them in sequence, but if you have neither time nor patience, then they each work individually. Part 2 does not assume that you have read Part 1, though it helps. Part 3 makes a lot more sense if you have already read Parts 1 and 2, but it isn't mandatory. Part 4, although just as firmly based on astrological principles as the other three, is deliberately intended as light relief.

The first part of the book deals with the theory behind the zodiac; it sets out the principles of astrology and enables you to see why Cancer is assigned the qualities it has, how the ruling planet system works, and what all the other signs are like in terms of motivation, so you can compare them to your own. There is a short and effective method given for assessing the aims and motives of other people. When you read Part 3 you will need to know a bit about the other signs, as you will be finding out that you have more to you than just the Cancer part you knew about.

The second part describes the essential Cancer. It shows you how there are different sorts of Cancerians according to where your birthday falls in the month, and shows how Cancerian energy is used differently in the Cancer as a child, adult, and parent.

Since you spend the greatest part of your life in dealing with other individuals, the way Cancer deals with relationships is treated in some detail. This is the largest section of the book.

The third part shows you a different kind of zodiac, and enables you to go into your own life in much greater detail. It isn't complicated, but you do need to think. It crosses the border between the kind of astrology you get in the magazines, and the sort of thing a real astrologer does. There's no reason why you can't do it yourself because, after all, you know yourself best.

The fourth part shows you the surface of being a Cancer, and how that zodiacal energy comes out in your clothes, your home, even your favourite food. The final item of this part actually explains the mechanics of being lucky, which you probably thought was impossible.

I hope that when you finish reading you will have a clearer view of yourself, and maybe like yourself a little more. Don't put the book away and forget about it; read it again in a few months' time—you will be surprised at what new thoughts about yourself it prompts you to form!

Note

Throughout this book, the pronouns 'he', 'him', and 'his' have been used to describe both male and female. Everything which applies to a male Cancerian applies to a female Cancerian as well. There are two reasons why I have not bothered to make the distinction: firstly, to avoid long-windedness; secondly, because astrologically there is no need. It is not possible to tell from a horoscope whether the person to whom it relates is male or female, because to astrology they are both living individuals full of potential.

BERNARD FITZWALTER

Part 1
How the Zodiac Works

1. The Meaning of the Zodiac

Two Times Two is Four; Four Times Three is Twelve

It is no accident that there are twelve signs in the zodiac, although there are a great many people who reckon themselves to be well versed in astrology who do not know the reasons why, and cannot remember ever having given thought to the principles behind the circle of twelve.

The theory is quite simple, and once you are familiar with it, it will enable you to see the motivation behind all the other signs as well as your own. What's more, you only have to learn nine words to do it. That's quite some trick—being able to understand what anybody else you will ever meet is trying to do, with nine words.

It works like this.

The zodiac is divided into twelve signs, as you know. Each of the twelve represents a stage in the life cycle of solar energy as it is embodied in the life of mankind here on our planet. There are tides in this energy; sometimes it flows one way, sometimes another, like the tides of the ocean. Sometimes it is held static, in the form of an object, and sometimes it is released when that object is broken down after a period of time. The twelve signs show all these processes, both physical and spiritual, in their interwoven pattern.

Six signs are used to show the flowing tide, so to speak, and six for the ebbing tide. Aries, Gemini, Leo, Libra, Sagittarius, and Aquarius are the 'flowing' group, and the others form the second group. You will notice at once that the signs alternate, one with the other, around the zodiac, so that the movement is maintained, and there is never a concentration of one sort of energy in one place. People whose Sun sign is in the first group tend to radiate their energies outwards from themselves. They are the ones who like to make the first move, like to be the ones to take command of a situation, like to put something of themselves into whatever they are doing. They don't feel right standing on the sidelines; they are the original have-a-go types. Energy comes out of them and is radiated towards other people, in the same way as the Sun's energy is radiated out to the rest of the solar system.

The people in the other signs are the opposite to that, as you would expect. They collect all the energy from the first group, keeping it for themselves and making sure none is wasted. They absorb things from a situation or from a personal contact, rather than contributing to it. They prefer to watch and learn rather than make the first move. They correspond to the Moon, which collects and reflects the energy of the Sun. One group puts energy out, one group takes it back in. The sum total of energy in the universe remains constant, and the two halves of the zodiac gently move to and fro with the tide of the energies.

This energy applies both to the real and concrete world of objects, as well as to the intangible world of thoughts inside our heads.

A distinction has to be made, then, between the real world and the intangible world. If this is done, we have four kinds of energy: outgoing and collecting, physical and mental. These four kinds of energy have been recognized for a long time, and were given names to describe the way they work more than two thousand years ago. These are the elements. All the energy in the cosmos can be described in the terms of these four: Fire, Earth, Air, Water.

Fire is used to describe that outgoing energy which applies to the real and physical world. There are three signs given to it: Aries, Leo, and Sagittarius. People with the Sun in any of these signs find themselves with the energy to get things going. They are at their best when making a personal contribution to a situation, and they expect to see some tangible results for their efforts. They are sensitive to the emotional content of anything, but that is not their prime concern, and so they tend to let it look after itself while they busy themselves with the actual matter in hand. Wherever you meet Fire energy in action, it will be shown as an individual whose personal warmth and enthusiasm are having a direct effect on his surroundings.

Earth is used to describe the real and physical world where the energies are being collected and stored, sometimes in the form of material or wealth. The three signs given to the element are Taurus, Virgo, and Capricorn. Where Fire energy in people makes them want to move things, Earth energy makes them want to hold things and stop them moving. The idea of touching and holding, and so that of possession, is important to these people, and you can usually see it at work in the way they behave towards their own possessions. The idea is to keep things stable, and to hold energy stored for some future time when it will be released. Earth Sun people work to ensure that wherever they are is secure and unlikely to change; if possible they would like the strength and wealth of their situation to increase, and will work towards that goal. Wherever you meet Earth energy in action, there will be more work being done than idle chat, and there will be a resistance to any kind of new idea. There will be money being made, and accumulated. The idea of putting down roots and bearing fruit may be a useful one to keep in mind when trying to understand the way this energy functions.

Air is used to describe outgoing mental energies; put more simply, this is communication. Here the ideas are formed in the mind of the individual, and put out in the hope that they can influence and meet the ideas of another individual; this is communication, in an abstract sense. Gemini, Libra, and Aquarius are all Air signs, and people with the Sun in those signs are very much concerned with communicating their energies to others. Whether anything gets done as a result of all the conversation is not actually important; if there is to be a concrete result, then that is the province of Fire or Earth energies. Here the emphasis is on shaping the concept, not the reality. There is an affinity with Fire energies, because both of them are outgoing, but other than that they do not cross over into each other's territory. Wherever you meet Air energy in action, there is a lot of talk, and new ideas are thrown up constantly, but there is no real or tangible result, no real product, and no emotional involvement; were there to be emotional content, the energies would be watery ones.

Water is the collection of mental energies. It is the response to communication or action. It absorbs and dissolves everything else, and puts nothing out. In a word, it is simply feelings. Everything emotional is watery by element, because it is a response to an outside stimulus, and is often not communicated. It is not, at least not in its pure sense, active or initiatory, and it does not bring anything into being unless transformed into energy of a different type, such as Fire. Cancer, Scorpio and Pisces are the Water signs, and natives of those signs are often moody, withdrawn, and uncommunicative. Their energy collects the energy of others, and keeps their mental responses to external events stored. They are not being sad for any particular reason; it is simply the way that energy works. It is quite obvious that they are not showing an outgoing energy, but neither have they anything tangible to show for their efforts, like the money and property which seem to accumulate around Earth people. Water people simply absorb, keep to themselves, and do not communicate. To the onlooker, this appears unexciting, but there again the onlooker is biased: Fire and Air energies only appreciate outgoing energy forms, Earth energies recognize material rather than mental energies, and other Water energies are staying private and self-contained!

We now recognize four kinds of energy. Each of these comes in three distinct phases; if one zodiac sign is chosen to represent each of these phases within an element, there would be twelve different kinds of energy, and that would define the zodiac of twelve, with each one showing a distinct and different phase of the same endless flow of energy.

The first phase, not surprisingly, is a phase of definition, where the energies take that form for the first time, and where they are at their purest; they are not modified by time or circumstance, and what they aim to do is to start things in their own terms. These four most powerful signs (one for each element, remember) are called cardinal signs: Aries, Cancer, Libra, Capricorn. When the Sun enters any of these signs, the seasons change; the first day of the Sun's journey through Aries is the first day of spring, and the Spring equinox; Libra marks the Autumnal equinox, while Cancer and Capricorn mark Mid-summer's Day and the shortest day respectively.

The second phase is where the energy is mature, and spreads itself a little; it is secure in its place, and the situation is well established, so there is a sort of thickening and settling of the energy flow. Here it is at its most immobile, even Air. The idea is one of maintenance and sustenance, keeping things going and keeping them strong. This stage is represented by Taurus, Leo, Scorpio, and Aquarius, and they are called, unsurprisingly, fixed signs. These four signs, and their symbols, are often taken to represent the four winds and the four directions North, South, East and West. Their symbols (with an eagle instead of a scorpion for Scorpio) turn up all over Europe as tokens for the avangelists Luke, Mark, John and Matthew (in that order).

The final phase is one of dissolution and change, as the energy finds itself applied to various purposes, and in doing so is changed into other forms. There is an emphasis on being used for the good, but being used up nonetheless. The final four signs are Gemini, Virgo, Sagittarius, and Pisces; in each of them the energies of their element are given back out for general use and benefit from where they had been maintained in the fixed phase. It is this idea of being used and changed which leads to this phase being called mutable.

Three phases of energy, then; one to form, one to grow strong and mature, and one to be used, and to become, at the end, something else. Like the waxing, full, and waning phases of the Moon.

The diagram on page 16 shows the twelve signs arranged in

their sequence round the zodiac. Notice how cleverly the cycle and phases interweave:

(a) Outgoing and collecting energies alternate, with no two the same next to each other;

(b) Physical ebb and flow are followed by mental ebb and flow alternately in pairs round the circle, meaning that the elements follow in sequence round the circle three times;

(c) Cardinal, fixed, and mutable qualities follow in sequence round the circle four times, and yet

(d) No two elements or qualities the same are next to each other, even though their sequences are not broken.

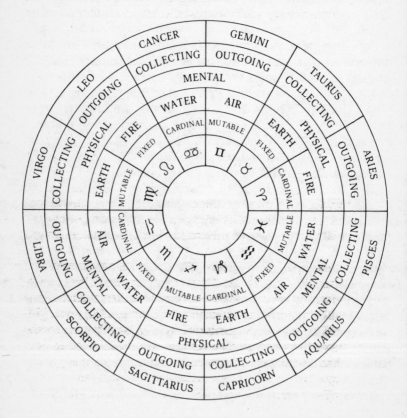

The interweaving is perfect. The zodiac shows all forms of energy, physical and mental, outgoing or incoming, waxing or waning, harmoniously forming a perfectly balanced unity when all the components are taken together. Humanity, as a whole, contains all the possibilities; each individual is a component necessary to the whole.

All this can be a bit long-winded when what you want is some way of holding all that information for instant recall and use, which is where the nine words come in.

If a single word is used for the kind of energy flow, and another two for the element and quality, then they can be used to form a sentence which will describe the way the energy is being used.

As a suggestion (use other words if they are more meaningful to you), try 'outgoing' and 'collecting' for the energy flows.

Next, for the elements:

Fire :	activity	(Aries, Leo, Sagittarius)
Earth:	material	(Taurus, Virgo, Capricorn)
Air :	communication	(Gemini, Libra, Aquarius)
Water:	feelings	(Cancer, Scorpio, Pisces)

And for the qualities:

Cardinal :	defining	(Aries, Cancer, Libra, Capricorn)
Fixed :	maintaining	(Taurus, Leo, Scorpio, Aquarius)
Mutable :	using	(Gemini, Virgo, Sagittarius, Pisces)

Now in answer to the question 'What is a Gemini doing?' and answer can be formed as 'He's outgoing, and he's using communication', which neatly encapsulates the motivation of the sign. All that you need to know about the guiding principles of a Gemini individual, no matter who he is, is in that sentence. He will never deviate from that purpose, and you can adapt your own actions to partner or oppose his intention as you please.

A Scorpio? He's collecting, and he's maintaining his feelings. An Arian? He's outgoing, and he's defining activity. And so on.

Those nine words, or some similar ones which you like better, can be used to form effective and useful phrases which describe the motivation of everybody you will ever meet. How different people show it is their business, but their motivation and purpose is clear if you know their birthday.

Remember, too, that this motivation works at all levels, from the immediate to the eternal. The way a Taurean conducts himself in today's problems is a miniature of the way he is trying to achieve his medium-term ambitions over the next two or three years. It is also a miniature of his whole existence: when, as an old man, he looks back to see what he tried to do and what he achieved, both the efforts and the achievement, whatever it is, can be described in the same phrase with the same three words.

2. The Planets and the Horseshoe

You will have heard, or read, about the planets in an astrological context. You may have a horoscope in a magazine which says that Mars is here or Jupiter is there, and that as a consequence this or that is likely to happen to you. Two questions immediately spring to mind: What do the planets signify? How does that affect an individual?

The theory is straightforward again, and not as complex as that of the zodiac signs in the previous chapter. Remember that the basic theory of astrology is that since the universe and mankind are part of the same Creation, they both move in a similar fashion, so Man's movements mirror those of the heavens. So far, so good. If you look at the sky, night after night, or indeed day after day, it looks pretty much the same; the stars don't move much in relationship to each other, at least not enough to notice. What do move, though, are the Sun and Moon, and five other points of light—the planets. It must therefore follow that if these are the things which move, they must be the things which can be related to the movements of Man. Perhaps, the theory goes, they have areas of the sky in which they feel more at home, where the energy that they represent is stronger; there might be other places where they are uncomfortable and weak, corresponding to the times in your life when you just can't win no matter what you do. The planets would then behave like ludo counters, moving round the heavens trying to get back to a home of their own colour, and then starting a new game.

The scheme sounds plausible, makes a sort of common sense, and is endearingly human; all hallmarks of astrological thought, which unlike scientific thought has to relate everything to the human experience. And so it is: the planets are given values to show the universal energy in different forms, and given signs of the zodiac as homes. Therefore your Sun sign also has a planet to look after it, and the nature of that planet will show itself strongly in your character.

The planets used are the Sun and Moon, which aren't really planets at all, one being a satellite and the other a star, and then Mercury, Venus, Mars, Jupiter, and Saturn. This was enough until the eighteenth century, when Uranus was discovered, followed in the subsequent two hundred years by Neptune and Pluto. Some modern astrologers put the three new planets into horoscopes, but it really isn't necessary, and may not be such a good idea anyway. There are three good reasons for this:

(a) The modern planets break up the symmetry of the original system, which was perfectly harmonious;

(b) The old system is still good enough to describe everything that can happen in a human life, and the modern planets have little to add;

(c) Astrology is about the relationship between the sky and a human being. An ordinary human being cannot see the outer planets on his own; he needs a telescope. We should leave out of the system such things as are of an extra-human scale or magnitude: they do not apply to an ordinary human. If we put in things which are beyond ordinary human capabilities, we cannot relate them to the human experience, and we are wasting our time.

In the diagram on page 21 the zodiac is presented in its usual form, but it has also been split into two from the start of Leo to the start of Aquarius. The right hand half is called the solar half, and the other one is the lunar half. The Sun is assigned to Leo because in the Northern hemisphere, where astrology started, August is when you feel the influence of the Sun most, especially in the Eastern Mediterranean, where the Greeks and the other early Western civilizations were busy putting the framework of astrology together in the second millennium BC. The Sun is important because it gives light. The Moon gives light too; it is reflected sunlight, but it is enough to see by, and this is enough to give the Sun and Moon the title of 'the Lights' in astrology. The Moon is assigned to Cancer, so that the two of them can balance and complement each other. From there, moving away from the Lights around the circle on both sides, the signs have the planets assigned to them starting with the fastest mover, Mercury, and continuing in decreasing order of speed. Saturn is the slowest mover of all, and the two signs opposite to

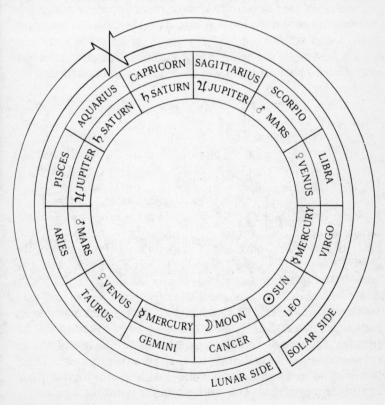

the Lights are both governed by that planet. The reasons for this apparent assymmetry will be explained in a little while. This arrangement is, of course, the horseshoe of the title to this chapter.

The Sun and Moon work in a similar fashion to the outgoing and collecting energies we noted earlier with the twelve signs. The Sun is radiant above all else; energy comes outwards from it, warming and energizing all those around it. Leo people, whose sign is the Sun's, work like this by being at the centre of a group of people and acting as inspiration and encouragement to them all. The Moon reflects the Sun's light, and energies of a lunar kind are directed inwards towards the core of the person. The two energies are necessarily linked; lunar people would starve without the solar folks' warmth, but the solar types need someone to radiate to or their purpose is unfulfilled.

The planets on each side of the horseshoe display their own energies in a solar or lunar way depending on which side of the pattern they are on.

Mercury and Venus form a pair, representing complementary but opposite ideas, which should be familiar by now. Mercury represents difference, and Venus stands for similarity.

Wherever anything new forms that is distinguishable from the background, then Mercury is there making it what it is, highlighting what makes it different. Anything separate is Mercurial, and words, since they are separate and can be strung together into millions of different combinations, are Mercurial too. Mercury is not a long-term influence; it notes things as being different for an instant, and then they become part of the establishment, and something else is new elsewhere. Because 'new' is an instantaneous state—that is, something can only be new once, and for a moment—Mercury is not associated with anything lasting, and its rapid motion as a planet leads to its being associated with the idea of speed. Virgo, Mercury's solar sign, is concerned with the changing of the shape of things ('collecting, using material' in our keyword system), while Gemini, the lunar sign, is concerned with reading and writing, and getting new ideas ('outgoing, using communication').

Venus does the reverse; it looks for that which is similar, finding points of contact to make relationships between common interests and energies. It likes to preserve the harmonies of life, and resents anything which might interrupt them. Love and affection are naturally Venusian, but so is music and all of the Arts, for the harmonies they contain. Expressed in a solar way, Venus is Libra, the maker of relationships; its lunar face is Taurus, emphasizing food and furnishings as things which give pleasure to the individual.

The next pair are Mars and Jupiter. Mars applies force from the outside to impose structure on a disordered universe, while Jupiter expands forcibly from the inside to give growth and wealth, inviting everyone else to join in.

Mars is pure force, energy in a straight line with a direction to go in. Anger and passion are both Martian, and so is lust, because they are all examples of great energy directed towards a given end. Note that Martian force is not necessarily strength, wealth, or know-how, just pure energy, which often boils over and needs controlling. Mars is the power in an athlete, and in an assassin too. It is also the power in a lover, because the urge to create is also the urge to pro-create, and if that energy fulfils its purpose then that creation takes place. Scorpio is its solar side, the power to control and create; in lunar form it is shown by Aries, as energy enjoyed for its own sake by its owner, with no purpose except to express it.

Jupiter is the spirit of expansion from within; not only does it oppose Mars' force from outside, it opposes Mars' physicality with its own mental emphasis. Jupiter develops the mind, then. As it does so, it develops all natural talents of an academic nature, and encourages movement, enquiry and travel to broaden experience and knowledge. The Solar expression of this is Sagittarius, where the centaur symbol is both a wise teacher and a free-roaming wild horse at the same time. Jupiter in a lunar sense is Pisces, where the imagination is developed to a greater extent than anywhere else, but used to provide an internal dream world for the owner's pleasure. Great sensitivity here, but the lunar energies are not of the sort to be expressed; rather other energies are *im*pressed on the Piscean mind.

Saturn is the last of the five planets. He stands alone, and if it is necessary to consider him as paired with anything it is with the Lights as an entity together. The Lights are at the centre of the system; Saturn is at its edge. They are the originators of the energies of the zodiac, and he is the terminator. Everything to do with limits and ends is his. He represents Time, and lots of it, in contrast to Mercury, which represented the instant. He represents the sum total of all things, and the great structures and frameworks of long-term endeavour. In solar form he is Capricorn, the representative of hard work, all hierarchies, and all rulers; in lunar form he is Aquarius, showing the horizontal structure of groups of people within society at different levels. Here he denies the activity of Mars, because society is too big for one person to change against the collective will, and he contains the expansion of Jupiter within himself. Venus and Mercury can neither relate to it nor make it change, because it is always the same, in the end.

The planets show important principles in action, the same as the zodiac does. You have probably noticed that the horseshoe of the planets and the ring of the zodiac say the same thing in a different way, and that is true about most things in astrology. It may be that the two systems interrelate and overlap because they are from the same source: after all, $3+2+2=7$, which is the planet's total, and $3x2x2=12$, which is the signs'. How you assign the elements and qualities, pairs of planets and lights is for you to decide. The joy of astrology, like all magic, is that it has you at the centre, and is made to fit its user's requirements. Now you know the principles, you can use it as you please, and as it seems relevant to you.

Part 2

Yourself—and Others

3. The Essential Cancer

All the energy in the zodiac is solar, but that solar energy takes many forms. It is moderated and distributed through the planetary energies until it finally shows in you, the individual. As a Cancer, the prime planetary energy is that of the Moon; you will be motivated by, and behave in the manner of, the energies of the Moon. To remind yourself of what that means, read the section on the Moon on page 22. As a sign of the zodiac, Cancer is a Cardinal Water sign. Remind yourself what that means by reading page 17. Now we have to see how those essential principles work when expressed through a person and his motivation.

What it Means to be a Cancer

You know what it is to be a Cancer, because you are one; but you probably don't know what it is that makes a Cancer the way he is, because you cannot stand outside yourself. You would have to be each of the other eleven signs in turn to understand the nature of the energy that motivates you. This essential energy is in every Cancerian, but it shows itself to different extents and in different ways. Because it is in every single Cancerian, it is universal rather than specific, and universal ideas tend to come in language which sounds a little on the woolly side. You will think that it isn't really about what makes you who you are, because you don't feel like that every day—or at least you think you don't. In fact, you feel like that all the time, but you don't notice it any more than you notice your eyes focusing, yet they do it all the time, and you see things the way you do because of it.

The first thing to note is that the zodiac is a circle, not a line with a beginning and an end. If it were a line, then Cancer would be a third of the way along, but that would be to miss the point; if the zodiac is a circle, then Cancer is a stage in an endlessly repeating cycle, and we will get a much better idea of what it is if we look to see where it came from, and where it is going.

The sign before Cancer is Gemini. In Gemini, the individual is concerned to notice things, think about them, and communicate his thoughts; he is eager to express the fact that he can think, and is able to assess his surroundings. He has noticed that there are other people in the world than himself, and he wants to see what they think about things, hence the communication that Geminis hold as their own special talent. Cancer is the next stage: assessing the reply. When the responses have been assessed, the individual is able to see how they affect his point of view: he forms an emotional response to his surroundings. After a while, he relies on his feelings more than his thoughts, and trusts to intuitive processes more than rational ones. This is Cancer. For Cancer, it is the emotions which are used to define the world. Emotional nourishment is needed, and actively sought. Relationships with the immediate family are used to provide a secure base for all the emotional requirements, leading to the development of feelings of caring, nurture, and belonging. All of these are the essential business of the Cancer phase of the zodiacal circle.

When the emotions are secure, confidence builds, and then the individual can act as a source of sustenance in himself for those around him. This is Leo, the next sign on from Cancer. As you can see, the sequence is one where emotions are formed and recognized, later to be output to others (in Leo); and where the sphere of interest widens from one individual, or perhaps two (Gemini) through a family group (Cancer) to a social group (Leo).

A Cancerian, you will remember from page 17, is 'collecting, and defining emotion'. There seems to be a paradox here: how can something as intangible as inward-flowing emotional energy (which is how we defined the element Water) have such a powerful and assertive word as 'defining' applied to it? Easy: the water springs from inside. It is the Cancerian who is the source and origin of the emotions he feels; everything that he comes into contact with causes more emotion to well up. It is not communicated; it does not flow in steady streams for the benefit of everybody else at large, but is kept inside until needed. Cancerians worry a great deal: to follow the analogy of the water, it is stored in underground reservoirs. Where the emotional energy is released, it appears as a caring impulse, the maternal instinct.

Biologically, Cancer corresponds to the stomach, and to the early stages of digestion (where food is responded to by gastric juices), and to the breasts. The relationship between the maternal urge, an outflow of self-generated emotion, the element of Water, and mother's milk isn't hard to understand.

There is a possessive side to a Cancerian; they are supposed to be moody and sensitive to hurt, yet they are also said to be protective and difficult to understand. All of these observations become more credible if the underlying motivation is examined. Since the Cancerian is seeking emotional stability and nourishment, he is bound to be protective of himself and his family, since they are what comforts him, and they need him to protect them in return. The flow of emotional interdependence round a family group is as real as the flow of the bloodstream to a Cancerian, and he needs emotional input of the reassuring variety as much as he needs to be able to output that energy in caring for something. The water flow needs to be maintained. Anything from outside which threatens to interrupt these essential activities is resisted. It is not in the Cancerian nature to counter-attack; the energy flow would have to be outgoing for that to be the case. Instead, there is absolute resistance. Once a Cancerian is resisting, then there is no way to move him other than by destroying him. You can't get into a crab except with a hammer, and that destroys the crab.

The Cancerian, then, is very possessive, but not of material things. It is important to realize this. There will be many material things to which he is very attached, but their value is not in what they are or what they are worth, or even what their use is, so much as the sentimental value they hold. The Cancerian is not what he owns, like the Taurian, or what he is seen to own, like the Capricorn, but what he feels. He will sacrifice all his belongings, if he has to; he will not sacrifice the people he loves.

Cancerian moodiness and over-sensitivity is simply due to an instinct for self-preservation. If every outside influence is known to produce an emotional response in the Cancerian, then he stays away from those things which affect his emotions in a way that he doesn't like. It is exactly the same as not eating those things which you know will upset your stomach.

One of the keys to understanding the way a Cancerian thinks, and how private he is, is to think of him as a box, or container. Whatever is inside the box, he regards as his, and cares for it. In return he is given emotional nourishment by the familiar and friendly responses of those he cares for. Everything that is outside the box he will resist, presenting an impassive and enduring exterior to the world; he is both protecting his own possessions and resisting any unwanted intrusions into his security and privacy. From the outside the box can look uninviting and uninteresting, especially to the outgoing signs, who tend to like organisms which, like themselves, radiate their energy to others. The inside of the box is warm and cosy, full of life and love. The alternative use of the box, where the outside is highly decorated, but the inside is empty, is found in Capricorn, the sign opposite to you.

To sum up, the Cancerian really is a lot like the animal in the zodiac picture, the crab. He is armoured against the world on the outside, to protect the essential parts within, which are soft and vulnerable. He is snappy when threatened, but unable to move very quickly to turn the situation to his advantage. When he does move, it is sideways, to avoid direct confrontation and action. Like the hermit crab, he is tied to his home environment, and likes it that way. His environment is water; it passes through him and around him the whole time, and he takes his nourishment from it.

Early, Middle or Late? The Decanates

Each of the zodiac signs is divided into degrees, like an arc of any other circle. Since a circle has 360 degrees, then each must be 30 degrees, since there are twelve signs. Each of the signs is further split into sections of ten degrees, called decanates. There are three decanates in each sign, and the one that your birthday falls in will tell you a little more about how that Cancerian energy actually works in you as an individual.

First Decanate (21–30 June)
This is the purest form of Cancer. There is a double helping of lunar energy here, and the emphasis is very much on the intuitive side of things. All sentiment and memory, plus combinations of the two, such as nostalgia, spring from this sector of the sign, and if your birthday is here, then the sentimental side of your character should be strongly developed. Allied to this is the sense of belonging and security that comes from being safe at home; this decanate is also assigned everything to do with hearth and home, so your own home is probably very cosy and much loved, somewhere that you feel is your retreat from the rest of the world. Motherhood and the feminine side of one's nature is, of course, a lunar thing, so with the Moon doubly active here, you should feel the urge to care for things and look after their needs as one of the most powerful you have. Do you look after stray kittens and sparrows with broken wings? On a slightly higher level, this lunar influence will show in an intuitive way of thinking, and a defensive attitude to go with it. That means that you know when you are right, because it feels right; but you don't know why it is so, though you're going to do it that way anyway. No amount of persuasion will deter you from these intuitive, internal, decisions. That's lunar energy.

Second Decanate (1–11 July)

Here the lunar energy is modified by that of Mars, giving a different frame of reference for all those internal emotions. There is a great feeling of tradition, history, and family in this decanate; the feeling that you are responsible for the creatures in your care is replaced by a feeling that you are responsible for the care of the traditions, history, and belongings of the family. You are likely to feel that you are the present holder of the office, so to speak, and that the care and continuance of the family's history is up to you. You are probably fascinated by what your grandparents did. Perhaps your home is furnished with some pieces of furniture from your mother's house, or your grandmother's; the sense of the family going back over the years is important to you, and provides both a sense of identity and a purpose for the future. You have a high regard for history, and particularly value old family possessions.

The Cancerian caring impulse here is not limited to the individual mother-and-child relationship of one generation, as it was in the first decanate; it is extended throughout time, both backwards into history and forwards into the future. These Cancerians are also fascinated by death and the processes of the end of life; to them, it is one of the joining links between generations of the same family—the other link being birth, of course, which is again a Cancerian matter.

Third Decanate (12–22 July)

The final decanate has the Moon's energies blended with those of Jupiter. Instead of extending the range of the caring impulse in time, as in the second decanate, it is extended in space. It looks to structures and properties; to organizations and large groups, especially large family groups; and to all definite structures and sets of rules. This decanate, and the people whose birthdays fall in it, looks upwards rather than down, whereas the first decanate looked inwards, and the second looked back rather than forwards. Here the Cancerian mind is trying to protect against unknown future threats by making solid defences. The Law, or any set of rules, is part of this way of thinking: if everybody keeps to the rules, then nobody should get hurt, and the Law is there to protect the helpless from harm. That's how the late Cancerian sees it. There is a need to see that things are properly and fairly set out, so that they will last, and be both secure and protective to their users—this is the prime concern of those born in this decanate. They take pride in their houses, especially their foundations: by now you can see why.

Three Phases of Life: Cancer as Child, Adult, Parent

The Cancer Child

The Cancerian child can look after himself, and in fact always does so—but in the opposite way to what that opening phrase implies. He goes through his early years carefully testing and feeling his way through life, with a deep distrust of whatever is new and potentially harmful to him. He is not at all adventurous— it is not in his nature to be so—and he sometimes has to be made to leave the house to go outside and play. He is always going to be concerned for his own security, and will flinch from anything which makes him at all uncertain of his safety or of whether he is going to like it. Cancerian children worry a great deal, mainly because early life offers so much that is new and different, with so many situations and behaviour patterns to be learned. If you remember that the Cancerian child will always try to give the right replies so that a positive emotional response is gained, then you will appreciate the difficulty in learning so many at once. The Cancerian child cannot 'play it by ear' or 'just be himself'; he is acutely conscious of what others think of him, and of the reaction they show to him. When troubled or unsure, he will always try to return to a situation which is familiar and comforting; often this means at home, close to a parent, and with a favourite object.

The older Cancerian child makes a perfect watchdog for his younger brothers and sisters; he can always see the danger in a deep pond, for example, or a busy road, and will make sure that the younger ones come to no harm, if only because he himself would not take such risks.

At school, Cancerian children are good at subjects which require retention, poor at those requiring expression; on the whole, then, they are good at history, poor at art and drama. They are not great team sportsmen; boisterous physical contact sports, such as rugby, may seem too hazardous to them.

The Cancerian Adult

By the time he is an adult, the Cancerian is quite practised at maintaining the ebb and flow of his emotions. Most of the time he keeps his emotions down under the surface, showing them only to those few individuals whom he trusts, and for whom he cares. He finds these people to be both a source and an outlet for emotional energies, and they are necessary for his continued health and well-being. He has a range of activities in which he feels 'comfortable'; by this he means that they are satisfying, that he can manage them without too much trouble, and they do not either threaten him or demand an excessive emotional reaction from him. If these needs are met, there is no reason for a Cancerian to seek out anything new to occupy him; if he does so, it is because he is being pushed. The push can be from external influences, or, if apparently self-motivated, from other planetary energies beside Cancerian ones; but the pure Cancerian would never seek outside challenge from a sense of adventure or boredom. (There is no such thing as a pure Cancerian, of course, nor a pure example of any other sign; when the Sun was in Cancer, the other planets were in other signs, making you an individual mixture; see the third part of the book.)

What the adult Cancerian looks for in his life is a secure situation that he can put roots down into and make his base. He tends to find this in a large organization; Cancerian entrepreneurs are rare indeed. Once in that organization, they work well; they abide by its rules, acquire areas of influence for themselves, look after those who are beneath them, and generally rise fairly quickly. They are the perfect company employees, and are often the ones who go from tea-boy to Managing Director within the same company. There are a surprising number of Cancerian generals and admirals: it is true that the armed forces are not exactly a caring profession, but they have a well-defined structure, and usually have a plan for any eventuality—and it is this internal security which attracts the Cancerian.

The Cancerian Parent

Cancerian parents are very caring and loving; they need little instruction in how to look after anything. They are masters at creating the warm home environment a child needs in his early years, and the child will never be deprived of affection and protection from parents such as these.

As the child grows, the Cancerian parent finds himself in a rather difficult position. He is still extending feelings of love and care towards the child, and will always do so, but he is threatened by the child's growing sense of individuality and independence. Cancerians always want things to stay in a stable pattern, and regard the home as the one place that this can be guaranteed to occur; a child who has his own ideas is a source of disruption to this pattern from within the home—a very worrying problem for the Cancerian parent. Cancerian parents worry as much for their children as they do for themselves; it always seems to escape them that children are fairly indestructible items with a strong instinct for self-preservation. Indeed, if this instinct is switched off by an over-protective home environment, then the child of Cancerian parents is considerably more at risk when outside the home than other children.

Cancerian fathers stabilize their emotional responses and opinions early, and so there is considerable 'generation gap' difficulty with teenage children. Cancerian mothers are rather better at this, identifying with the home rather than with the child and becoming serene matriarchs as the generations of their families unfold below them.

4. Cancer Relationships

How Zodiacal Relationships Work

You might think that relationships between two people, described in terms of their zodiac signs, might come in 144 varieties; that is, twelve possible partners for each of the twelve signs. The whole business is a lot simpler than that. There are only seven varieties of relationship, although each of those has two people in it, of course, and the role you play depends on which end of the relationship you are at.

You may well have read before about how you are supposed to be suited to one particular sign or another. The truth is usually different. Cancerians are supposed to get on with Scorpios and Pisceans, and indeed they do, for the most part, but it is no use reading that if you have always found yourself attracted to Aquarians, is it? There has to be a reason why you keep finding Aquarians attractive, and it is not always to do with your Sun sign; other factors in your horoscope will have a lot to do with it. The reason you prefer people of certain signs as friends or partners is because the relationship of your sign to theirs produces the sort of qualities you are looking for, the sort of behaviour you find satisfactory. When you have identified which of the seven types of basic relationship it is, you can see which signs will produce that along with your own, and then read the motivation behind it explained later on in more detail in

'The Cancerian Approach to Relationships' and the individual you can make much progress together.

Look at the diagram on page 16. All you have to do is see how far away from you round the zodiacal circle your partner's Sun sign is. If they are Sagittarius, they are five signs in front of you. You are also, of course, five signs behind them, which is also important, as you will see in a little while. If they are Aries, they are three signs behind you, and you are three signs in front of them. There are seven possibilities: you can be anything up to six signs apart, or you can both be of the same sign.

Here are the patterns of behaviour for the seven relationship types.

Same sign

Somebody who is of the same sign as you acts in the same way that you do, and is trying to achieve the same result for himself. If your goals permit two winners, this is fine, but if only one of you can be on top, you will argue. No matter how temperamental, stubborn, devious, or critical you can be, they can be just the same, and it may not be possible for you to take the same kind of punishment you hand out to others. In addition, they will display every quality which really annoys you about yourself, so that you are constantly reminded of it in yourself as well as in them. Essentially, you are fighting for the same space, and the amount of tolerance you have is the determining factor in the survival of this relationship.

One sign apart

Someone one sign forward from you acts as an environment for you to grow in. In time, you will take on those qualities yourself. When you have new ideas, they can often provide the encouragement to put them into practice, and seem to have all your requirements easily available. Often, it is this feeling that they already know all the pitfalls that you are struggling over which can be annoying; they always seem to be one step ahead of you, and can seemingly do without effort all the things which you have to sweat to achieve. If the relationship works well, they are helpful to you, but there can be bitterness and jealousy if it doesn't.

Someone one sign back from you can act as a retreat from the pressures of the world. They seem to understand your particular needs for rest and recovery, whatever they may be, and can usually provide them. They can hold and understand your innermost secrets and fears; indeed, their mind works best with the things you fear most, and the fact that they can handle these so easily is a great help to you. If the relationship is going through a bad patch, their role as controller of your fears gets worrying, and you will feel unnerved in their presence, as though they were in control of you. When things are good, you feel secure with them behind you.

Two signs apart
Someone two signs forward from you acts like a brother or sister. They are great friends, and you feel equals in each other's company; there is no hint of the parent-child or master-servant relationship. They encourage you to talk, even if you are reticent in most other company; the most frequently heard description of these relationships is 'We make each other laugh'. Such a partner can always help you put into words the things that you want to say, and is there to help you say them. This is the relationship that teenagers enjoy with their 'best friend'. There is love, but it does not usually take sexual form, because both partners know that it would spoil the relationship by adding an element of unnecessary depth and weight.

Someone two signs behind you is a good friend and companion, but not as intimate as somebody two signs forward. They are the sort of people you love to meet socially; they are reliable and honest, but not so close that things become suffocatingly intense. They stop you getting too serious about life, and turn your thoughts outwards instead of inwards, involving you with other people. They stop you from being too selfish, and help you give the best of yourself to others. This relationship, then, has a cool end and a warm end; the leading sign feels much closer to his partner than the trailing sign does, but they are both satisfied by the relationship. They particularly value its chatty quality, the fact that it works even better when in a group, and its tone of affection and endearment rather than passion and obsession.

Three signs apart
Someone three signs in front of you represents a challenge of some kind or another. The energies of the pair of you can never run parallel, and so must meet at some time or another. Not head on, but across each other, and out of this you can both make something strong and well established which will serve the two of you as a firm base for the future. You will be surprised to find how fiercely this person will fight on your behalf, or for your protection; you may not think you need it, and you will be surprised that anybody would think of doing it, but it is so nonetheless.

Someone three signs behind you is also a challenge, and for the same reasons as stated above; from this end of the relationship, though, they will help you achieve the very best you are capable of in a material sense. They will see to it that you receive all the credit that is due to you for your efforts, and that everyone thinks well of you. Your reputation is their business, and they will do things with it that you could never manage yourself. It's like having your own P.R. team. This relationship works hard, gets results, and makes sure the world knows it. It also looks after itself, but it needs a lot of effort putting in.

Four signs apart
Someone four signs forward from you is the expression of yourself. All the things you wanted to be, however daring, witty, sexy, or whatever, they already are, and you can watch them doing it. They can also help you to be these things. They do things which you think are risky, and seem to get away with them. There are things you aim towards, sometimes a way of life that you would like to have, which these people seem to be able to live all the time; it doesn't seem to worry them that things might go wrong. There are lots of things in their life which frighten you, which you would lie awake at nights worrying

about, which they accept with a child's trust, and which never go wrong for them. You wish you could be like that.

Someone four signs behind you is an inspiration to you. All the things you wish you knew, they know already. They seem so wise and experienced, and you feel such an amateur; luckily, they are kind and caring teachers. They are convincing, too. When they speak, you listen and believe. It's nice to know there's somebody there with all the answers. This extraordinary relationship often functions as a mutual admiration society, with each end wishing it could be more like the other; unfortunately, it is far less productive than the three-sign separation, and much of its promise remains unfulfilled. Laziness is one of the inherent qualities of a four-sign separation; all its energies are fulfilled, and it rarely looks outside itself for something to act upon. Perhaps this is just as well for the rest of us.

Five signs apart

Someone five signs ahead of you is your technique. You know what you want to do; this person knows how to do it. He can find ways and means for you to do what you want to be involved in, and he can watch you while you learn and correct your mistakes. They know the right way to go about things, and have the clarity of thought and analytical approach necessary if you are to get things clear in your mind before you get started

Someone five signs behind you is your resource. Whenever you run out of impetus or energy, they step forward and support you. When you're broke, they lend you money, and seldom want it returned. When you need a steadying hand because you think you've over-reached yourself, they provide it. All this they do because they know that it's in their best interest as well as yours, to help you do things, and to provide the material for you to work with. You can always rely on them for help, and it's nice to know they will always be there. They cannot use all their talent on their own; they need you to show them how it should be done. Between you, you will use all that you both have to offer effectively and fully, but it is a relationship of cooperation and giving; not all the zodiac signs can make it work well enough.

Six signs apart

Someone six signs apart from you, either forwards or backwards, is both opponent and partner at the same time. You are both essentially concerned with the same area of life, and have the same priorities. Yet you both approach your common interests from opposite directions, and hope to use them in opposite ways. Where one is private, the other is public, and where one is self-centred, the other shares himself cheerfully. The failings in your own make-up are complemented by the strengths in the other; it is as if, between you, you make one whole person with a complete set of talents and capabilities. The problem with this partnership is that your complementary talents focus the pair of you on a single area of life, and this makes for not only a narrow outlook, but also a lack of flexibility in your response to changes. If the two of you are seeing everything in terms of career, or property, or personal freedom, or whatever, then you will have no way to deal effectively with a situation which cannot be dealt with in those terms. Life becomes like a seesaw; it alternates which end it has up or down, and can sometimes stay in balance; but it cannot swing round to face another way, and it is fixed to the ground so that it does not move.

These are the only combinations available, and all partnerships between two people can be described as a version of one of the seven types. It must be remembered, though, that some of the roles engendered by these dispositions of sign to sign are almost impossible to fulfil for some of the signs, because their essential energies, and the directions they are forced to take by the planets behind them, drive them in ways which make it too difficult. To form a relationship based on sharing and acceptance is one thing: to do it when you are governed by a planet like Mars is somethings else. Even when the relationship can form, the sort of approach produced by, say, Jupiter, is a very different thing from that produced by Venus.

The next thing you must consider, then, is how you, as a Cancerian, attempt relationships as a whole, and what you try to find in them. Then you must lay the qualities and outlook of each of the twelve signs over the roles they must play in the seven relationship types, and see whether the pair of you manage to make the best of that relationship, or not.

The seven relationship types are common to all the signs, relating to all the other signs. You can use your understanding of them to analyse and understand the relationship between any pair of people that you know, whether or not they are Cancerian; but to see how the characters fit into the framework in more detail, you will need to look at the individual compatibilities, of which just the Cancerian ones are given in this book.

The Cancerian Approach to Relationships

All relationships are personal ones to a Cancerian. This sounds obvious, I know, but not all of the other signs feel so personally involved with the people they meet as a Cancerian does. It is quite possible for a Capricorn or an Aquarian to have a working partnership with somebody that they don't really like at all. As long as the partnership serves its purpose, which may well be a commercial one, then they don't mind what the other person is actually like.

Cancerians don't think this way; in fact they can't think this way. Since they bring their emotions and intuition into play every time they meet somebody, and since their future actions are influenced by what they think of people, then every relationship, business or social, is conducted on the level of a personal friendship. Business relationships thus stand or fall on the strength of the affection the Cancerian has for his partner.

It is not possible for a Cancerian to remain cool towards another person. If he feels sympathy and affection, then he will want to share some of his feelings and care for the well-being of the other; this will show in a variety of ways, from simple sympathy in difficulties to actively helping. In a business environment this can take the form of placing orders with suppliers or contractors whom the Cancerian likes and trusts rather than new and unknown people. If the Cancerian feels antipathy and discomfort in somebody's company, then he will shield himself from that person, and appear reserved and uncommunicative. Either way, there is no middle ground; the Cancerian forms an opinion of somebody based on his personal reaction to them, and this is what guides his behaviour from then on.

What does a Cancerian want out of a relationship? The best way of finding out is probably to look at the energies of the Moon, which is the essential principle of Cancerianism. Have a look at page 22, and page 12 too.

Lunar energy needs solar energy first. What a Cancerian wants from a relationship is for somebody to offer him warmth, affection, the glow of his own personality in companionship. This is similar to the Sun pushing out light and heat to anything within range. When this flow of personal warmth is established, the Cancerian absorbs it, and generates within himself his own sort of complementary energy as a reflection of the incoming warmth. This new energy is then made available to the other person to use and enjoy. It is similar to moonlight; it is a much softer product altogether, more soothing and reassuring. It is quieter and cooler, and the great thing about it is that it can be stored, which the other sort cannot.

This caring sort of energy is not easy to see when there are a lot of people around radiating their own warmth and enthusiasm, just as you cannot see the stars in the daytime. When things go wrong, however, and the person with the ebullient energy is feeling less than radiant, the Cancerian's stored lunar energy is there to care for him, and he feels better. Cancerians need to care for people, and to have that caring recognized; they do this to express all the lunar energies formed in them by having non-lunar people radiate their own warmth towards them.

What the Cancerian looks for in a relationship, then, is to establish the circular flow of lunar energy. He needs somebody to offer him warmth and affection, and when he has that, he will reflect that warmth back as care and protection. This effect becomes more noticeable, as we have seen, when the initial source of warmth falters or fails for any reason.

As a friend, a Cancerian is constant and reliable. Once the

friendship has formed, there is very little that would induce the Cancerian to break it off, because to do so would mean not caring for somebody he cared for in the past; a very un-Cancerian thing. Any variation in the level of closeness will be compensated for by the Cancerian, who will regard this as one of the little 'down' phases that all people go through, and provide more of his caring gestures to make up the difference. Even when the friendship is distant, and the friends hardly ever see each other, the Cancerian keeps his end of the bargain, so to speak, with letters and Christmas cards. Birthdays and anniversaries will be remembered. This particular practice always astounds the distant non-Cancerian friend: it shouldn't. It arises because to the friend, the important part of a friendship is likely to be something like physical companionship or a shared goal, but to the Cancerian the important part is the sentiment. Consequently, sentimental items like birthdays are unforgettable to the Cancerian, and they are remembered accordingly.

Cancerians take friendship seriously, and are hurt when a friend is inconsiderate. They will forgive, of course, and they would never show how much they have been hurt, but they do not forget very easily, and they can suffer a long time. Friendships are important to the Cancer soul; people from the other signs have a much more flippant attitude, and may think nothing of breaking friendships when they are no longer convenient or attractive. Treating friendships so lightly is very wounding to Cancerians, and it hurts the more because they dare not show it. Of course, if they do not show it, then the rest of the world thinks no harm has been done, and a vicious circle is set up. This is why Cancer crabs have hard shells, perhaps.

Marriage is virtually a Cancerian institution. It is probably the desire to make permanent roots out of a rewarding friendship which drives Cancerians to marry; whatever it is, they suit marriage very well. It gives them a solid framework, reasonably secure against personal attack; they can build a family unit from it, and from that they can form links to other branches of their own families to provide emotional security and mutual support. Cancerians are devoted to their spouses; they are tenacious fighters for what is theirs anyway, and once married will defend mutual interests just as fiercely.

In sexual relationships Cancer is stronger than you might think: it is a cardinal sign, remember, so it defines its own territory. The relationship will be at least as intense on an emotional level as it is on a physical one, probably more so: the Moon is the great feminine principle, and is an exact match and partner for the most powerful masculine elements her partners have to offer.

Individual Compatibilities Sign by Sign

All relationships between the signs work in the ways described earlier in 'How Zodiacal Relationships Work' (page 35). In addition to that, descriptions of how a Cancerian attempts to form a relationship with someone from each of the twelve signs are given below. I have tried to show not what a Virgo, for example, is like, but what a Cancerian sees him as, and how he sees you. Each individual Virgo looks very different, of course, but their motivation is the same, and these descriptions are meant to help you understand what you are trying to do with them, and how they are trying to handle you. As usual, the words he and his can be taken to mean she and her, since astrology makes no distinctions in sex here.

Cancer-Aries
On the surface this relationship would appear to have little to recommend it: the blazing energy of Aries and the careful nature of Cancer do not have a lot in common. In actual practice, this pairing is much more successful than it looks at first sight, and often becomes a very strong bond indeed.

In some ways, it is precisely because you are so different that this union works so well. Aries is the embodiment of Mars, the masculine sexual principle, and Cancer is the embodiment of the Moon, the feminine principle. There is thus a natural union here: the masculinity of the one is the perfect partner for the femininity of the other. It does not matter if the Arian is female and the Cancerian male, nor indeed if they are both of the same sex: the energy flow is just the same.

The Arian is very direct, very energetic, and very simple in his approach to problems. In order to achieve his purposes, he throws himself at his tasks with all his energy, and usually succeeds just by the force of his attack. He is not very sophisticated in his analysis of the situation, though, and if he is thwarted for any reason he feels confused, unable to see why things should be this way. This is a rather childlike approach, and as with children it is beneficial if someone is on hand to dry the tears. Cancerians fill this role admirably: there is something about the stunned helplessness of an Arian who has just failed to do something which appeals to the caring instinct in the Cancerian soul.

The Arian can play the role of the child to the Cancerian mother, and the arrangement is emotionally satisfying to both sides. Arians understand things best if they are direct and uncomplicated; the care and sympathy generated by a Cancerian are both of these things; what's more, they are not the sort of thing an Arian can produce on his own, and he is grateful to have his emotional needs looked after by someone who is much better at it than he is.

Both of the signs are cardinal: therefore both people are the sort who prefer to make the decisions about what form their life takes, unlike the fixed-sign people who prefer to fit into a ready-made role. One of the differences between you, though, is that the Arian really does make the decisions about the form of his life, whereas the Cancerian is often inhibited from doing so. The very effectiveness of the Arian approach thrills the Cancerian; in partnership with Aries, he gets the power he needs, and his ambitions start to become realities. It's really simple physics: water (Cancer) is a slow if steady force, but if you heat the water with fire (Aries) you get steam—and you can drive locomotives with that!

As a friendship, this is one of the most open you could wish for. Neither of you is in the slightest underhand or dishonest— Cancer because your emotions won't let you be, and Aries because he simply can't be—it wouldn't occur to him! Although you may sometimes be upset by the force of his temper when you disagree, you are grateful for his honesty, and you also know that his rage doesn't last long. You are more likely to be hurt when he asserts his independence, and rushes off in pursuit of some new adventure, leaving you behind. You have to understand that this is not deliberate cruelty, just more youthful boisterousness, and you must learn to live with that as mothers learn to live with sons who behave in a similar way.

As lovers, you have a great deal to offer one another on a very high level; it's the meeting of the masculine and feminine principles again. You will have to accept his occasional lack of tenderness, and realize, too, that you sometimes want to be with him more than he wants to be with you. Fire sign people are like that: you can't hold them down. It will break your heart before it breaks his, so accept it.

As marriage or business partners you could do very well indeed. Remember that you may share the same goals, but your methods and priorities in working will be wildly different, so allow for this. Aries will provide the drive, Cancer the care and support; but to Cancer, Aries will appear reckless, while to Aries Cancer seems a timid worrier. You appreciate each other's efforts, though: that's the key to it.

Cancer-Taurus

One of the easiest friendships in the whole zodiac, for the Moon has a particular affinity with the sign of the Bull. The whole relationship has something of an organic quality to it, though: intuition and the hidden pull of the tides are present in this pairing, giving almost nothing which an outsider can put his finger on, especially if he is looking for an outgoing and enterprising partnership which is visibly lively. No, this one works below the surface: this one is where you instinctively feel right with the other without knowing why, and without having to ask. You protect and nourish each other, and you never expose each other to anything which might worry or disconcert you. You feel safe in each other's presence. You don't stimulate or challenge each other: instead, you comfort and reassure each other, defending each other against anyone and everyone who is harsher and less sensitive.

What is the secret of this closeness? It is to do with something called exaltation, one of astrology's little nooks and crannies. What happens is that each planet has a sign, not usually the one it rules, where its energies are particularly well received. In the case of Cancer and the Moon, this sign is Taurus. Since the Moon is particularly happy in Taurus, then it follows that a lunar person, a Cancerian, will be particularly happy in the presence of a Taurean.

The key is in the feminine and nurturing side of both signs. The Moon is very receptive; it takes the energy of the other planets, and especially the Sun, and looks after it, modifying it and softening it as it goes. This 'looking after' process is connected with natural cycles of growth, and with natural processes of nourishment. All of this is very similar to the Taurean's emphasis on feeding and growth. Both signs are receptive and supportive: both of them give rise to a sensitive and maternal attitude in people. True, Taurus is more concerned with purely material things, and Cancer is far more able to make major changes in life, but there is much in common in their outlook. Both appreciate security, and are essentially shy in their approach to new people. As a consequence, the relationship will be very close and emotionally satisfying for both of you, but it will be very much a closed affair as far as outsiders are concerned; you see no need to share yourselves with anybody else, because you feel quite happy in each other's company.

The lunar emphasis of this relationship will mean that you don't develop anything new out of it. This isn't the kind of friendship which produces new ideas, provides mutual encouragement for pioneering achievement, or strikes sparks from the meeting of two minds which can be used to kindle bigger fires. Not at all. This is the one which works as a closed-circuit retreat for both of you. It can lead to a sort of smugness, or to fits of giggles at private jokes nobody else understands, or to a tight, defensive cliquiness, depending on other factors in the horoscopes of the two individuals.

As friends, you comfort each other and support each other: as lovers, you attempt to possess each other. The Taurean thinks that the Cancerian is his personal property, and the Cancerian feels that he has an absolute right to the Taurean's time and affections. Whilst this kind of devotion is useful in cementing a relationship, it is possible to have too much of a good thing, and there is too much of it here. Eventually you will stifle the very real joy of the early days of the affair with feelings of obligation and suspicion; neither of you is willing to let go, of course. Perhaps this friendship is best not taken to so intense a level.

As business partners, you will be industrious, but cautious; a third person is needed to give impetus and contribute fresh ideas.

As a marriage, this will definitely have the emphasis on a secure home. You will be very considerate of each other's needs, and as a safe base from which to raise a family it could hardly be bettered. It will be very static, though; you had better not have any secret desires to move around or make far-reaching changes—this isn't the sort of marriage to accommodate them.

Cancer–Gemini

This is the most difficult friendship the Cancerian ever makes. The sign before your own is always difficult to handle; in one sense you always feel that you have grown past that sort of behaviour, but in another sense you are afraid that you find it rather appealing. A person from that sign seems to know all your weak points in advance, but despite that terrrible possibility you find them irresistible in an odd sort of way.

The essential problem is that you don't think you can actually trust a Gemini. They are never short of things to say—indeed, they think aloud at times—but what they say isn't necessarily what they believe. Belief is an emotional addition to a logical conclusion, and as such is not part of the Gemini mind. They are also likely to change their minds very quickly, as soon as another way of looking at something occurs to them, and the apparent conflict between their opinion now and their opinion yesterday does not bother them one bit.

On the other hand, you react quite strongly to what they say, and will react just as strongly to the amended version too. Constantly changing your reactions and beliefs is both wearying and worrying for you, and after a while you begin to wonder whether you can believe any of it at all. Your attempts to provide the right replies when the conversation changes will irritate both of you; Gemini will find your insistence on sticking to one thing at a time very tedious, while you find his constantly changing point of view rather devious. Neither of you are right.

You are, of course facing the world in different directions. Gemini has a very low emotional level, but a very high intellectual level, and you are just the opposite. It would be easier if you were both cardinal, or both Water, but in fact everthing about you is different. Perhaps the most difficult thing of all for you to understand is how the Gemini never takes anything at all seriously, and how the idea of putting others first never enters his head. In his turn, the most difficult thing for him to understand about you is that you feel rather than think, and place sentiment above almost all other values.

If your acquaintance is to develop into friendship, you will be need to be ready for his changes of mood and opinion. You will also need to be ready for his complete inability to understand your values—but that doesn't mean that he isn't interested in your point of view; be ready to tell him about all you feel (not easy for a Cancerian, I know) and you will maintain his interest in you. In return, you will be vastly entertained, and swept along with him as he lives his life as fast as he can; perhaps you will enjoy scandalizing yourself as you watch him get away with what you know you couldn't.

You will need the same readiness to accept his changeable nature if you are to become lovers. He will take his freedom when it suits him—not to hurt you, but because it never occurs to him that you would expect any other sort of behaviour. He is completely blind to the devotion with which you cling to him, and can have no inkling of how deeply you are wounded when he decides to try something (or somebody) else for a while. Yet you do know, don't you, deep down, that his freedom from ties, his autonomy, is just what you find so attractive?

As business partners you would do better looking after different sides of the company, and as marriage partners a similar division of labour would be the best policy. You will have to adopt his practice of logical appraisal rather than pure gut reaction to solve major problems together, but he must learn to express the emotion he secretly fears if you are to live together.

Cancer–Cancer

A cautious and considerate combination. You might think that having two lunar people together would make for a close and understanding realtionship, but it isn't anything like as comfortable as the Cancer–Taurus union.

Both of you go in phases, like the Moon. Sometimes you want one thing, sometimes you feel that you've seen enough of it and would like a change. You are often tired by the effort of dealing with people who are not particularly comfortable to be with, and you would like a rest, some time to yourself, some time to be private. Sometimes you want somebody to warm you and share their successes, whilst shielding you from any unpleasantness. What happens if your partner is just as changeable, but the two of you are out of phase?

The chances of you being in exactly the same phase are small, although two women living or working together will align their physical lunar cycles, as is well known; the problem doesn't get any better even if you are aligned, though. If both of you need somebody to restore your energies, you are stuck, aren't you?

In forming this relationship, as with all relationships between two people of the same sign, you must remember that you are both motivated by the same energies, and will be trying to achieve the same result. If that result comes from a one-way transaction, so that you gain something at their expense, then obviously one of you is going to be disappointed: in fact you both are, if you think about it. On the other hand, the positive talents that you bring to the relationship are doubled since you are both contributing, but that may not necessarily redress the balance. After all, if you make cake with twice as much flour and only half as many eggs, you still get cake, but it doesn't taste quite the way you expected it to.

Both of you like to feel that you are quite sure how the other person is likely to behave. If the other person hides his feelings a little, or is uncommunicative and shy, as Cancerians often are, then you may have a little difficulty anticipating their moves. This is even more pronounced, of course, if they have changed their mood since the last time you met.

Both of you need, ideally, somebody to act as a Sun to your Moon, somebody who is going to be able to light up the partnership with his own cheerful personality and enthusiasm. If you have to play this role for each other, you are going to feel that it is something of a responsibility, and in playing that role to the best of your ability (as you will—you never give less than your best when somebody depends on you) you will feel that you are giving out more than you are getting back, which will worry you a little. Sometimes you will be unable to muster the energy and enthusiasm required to lift the pair of you because you are uncertain of what to do for the best: it is at times like this when the partnership starts to sink. The further it sinks, the more concerned you get, and the more you worry, but as I hope you can see, that's precisely the wrong sort of energy needed on these occasions.

On the positive side, you do sympathize with each other's misfortunes and cares, and can provide real support for each other in the way that only Cancerians know that they need—and that is a very big plus mark for this particular pairing. If you have mutual interests and shared goals, you can use them as an anchor point to haul yourselves out of the bad patches with, and you can make much progress together.

As lovers, you will be supremely sensitive to each other's needs, knowing as few other signs do that love exists on many levels at once, and the ones that matter most to the Cancerian are the invisible ones. You will also think that you cannot possibly have so close a relationship again. Cancerians feel this way about anybody they trust, and will hang on to people they love far longer than they should. If it really isn't working, for heaven's sake let go.

As business partners, or as marriage partners, you will never lack care and concern, though you may well lack flexibility and a sense of enterprise. Try to see the grand scheme rather than the immediate problem.

Cancer–Leo

This partnership is almost as difficult as the Gemini one, though the difficulty is of a different kind. Here you have all the solar energy that you could want; Leo is the embodiment of solar power. You always say that you want somebody who can provide you with warmth; here he is. Why is it so difficult to form the relationship you want?

It is something to do with the fact that this is one of those pairings where both the element and the quality are different: you even represent different universes (Water and Fire: imaginary and tangible). It certainly seems as though you are a universe apart at times.

The Leo is an energy source all to himself, generating energy and radiating it outwards. He likes to feel that he is at the centre of things, and he likes things to go his way. Since he is usually the prime mover in any situation, they usually do. Thus by putting himself at the centre of a small group of people, and becoming their natural focus and source of inspiration, he achieves what he wants, and feels satisfied.

To you, this seems remarkably pompous. You feel that he does what he does not because he cares for the people who surround him, but to reassure his own vanity. You are right, of course, but are you sure that you don't care for those around you because you welcome their appreciation of your efforts, or because it enables you to keep up with what's going on? It is very difficult to assign blame in the business of planetary energies: in the end they work to everyone's benefit.

There is a mutual antipathy between you which needs to be overcome, and it springs from the fact that the two signs follow each other in the zodiacal sequence. Leo would rather enjoy the company of his friends and supporters than worry about his motives for doing so, and he sees your careful, inward-looking attitude as a criticism of his happy state. He is trying to keep things as they are, with everybody smiling: he is, after all, a fixed sign. He knows that he benefits from everyone's admiration, but they benefit from his warmth and generosity, so why not? In addition, because he believes that things can be made to happen by applying energy to them, he does so. If he stopped believing this, stopped being generous, and started to worry about whether anybody really liked him, he would be slipping back down the zodiacal scale towards Cancerianism, which he tries always to avoid.

On your part, you see him as prodigally wasteful of his energies. He also seems to have no sensitivity to the emotional climate of the moment. Nor should he, if you think about it, because he is not reacting to the thoughts of others, he is radiating energy and enthusiasm outwards from himself. Still, you see him in your terms; he seems brash and insensitive to you. He gives out personal information, which you keep very close to you indeed; how could he be so stupid? Simple: to him it isn't stupid. He is simply putting more of himself on display. You may not admit it to yourself, but you find this secretly wonderful. If only you could have the sort of confidence, that invulnerability to the opinions of others, the unshakable belief in your own capability, and not the least the sheer generosity of the Leo. All this is something you can only aim for, but never achieve: it is the exclusive preserve of the next sign from your own, and you must stay where you are in the circle of the signs.

The way to form a friendship with a Leo is to surrender to their generosity. If he wants to buy you expensive presents, accept them. There is no emotional blackmail going on—they are genuinely generous people. All you have to do is recognize them as the central figure in your life, which is the difficult bit for you. You will have to let them have their own way, and you won't like that either. Relax— there is no malice here; you are quite safe.

Whatever your relationship with a Leo, be it as lovers,

business partners, or whatever, keep your worries to yourself. To express them suggests that you doubt his abilities, and annoys him. Besides, you have no need to worry—everything goes right for a Leo.

Cancer–Virgo

This is a lovely union. You are complementary to each other; you each fill in the bits that the other hasn't got. Cancer is very emotional in its outlook, and spends most of its time dealing with the world of feelings, to which it applies care and understanding. Virgo is much more concerned with the physical world, and spends most of its time dealing with methods and materials, which it does with care and understanding. You can see at once that there is great similarity of approach.

Virgoans share your belief that little things matter. When a Virgo comes into contact with something new he spends a lot of time with it, looking at it, thinking about it, getting to know it. He spends a lot of time actually holding it, feeling it, running his hands over it—a Virgo needs to get to know the shape of things. Nor is he likely to do this just once: repeated activity is something very important to the Virgoan mind. What is happening is that the Virgo is building up a sense of how he reacts to the physical nature of something, in the same way as you work with the emotional nature of something. You understand very well the idea of doing something more than once—there is a sort of reassurance in being able to get things right again and again. 'Patience' and 'practice' are Virgoan words, and you have little difficulty in understanding the motivation behind them.Virgoans like to understand things fully, right down to the component parts. They do things in a methodical and patient way, always trying to see how the whole thing fits together, and gaining satisfaction from that understanding. In short, they handle people's external natures and movements the same way you handle their internal natures and movements, and you recognize a mind which works in a similar fashion to your own.

To the Virgoan, you seem to have the right ideas. The quality that they see as the most evident in your nature is that of caring.

Not only caring for other people, which they see as an attempt to assimilate the other person into yourself (they may be right at that—had you thought of it that way?), but caring that things are done properly. Whilst this is true, it is being looked at from two very different angles: you care about details because you want the things in your care to behave in an entirely predictable way, while they care about details because they can only understand the whole by noting all the parts and then adding them up.

As friends, you should be able to appreciate both the similarities and the differences of your points of view. Remember that the Virgo's way of looking at things starts with the details and works outwards, so when they remark on some small point about you it isn't the criticism it would be coming from anybody else—it simply denotes interest and an attempt to communicate.

As lovers, you will take some time to get going. This is because of the Virgo's inability to see things on the grand scale; he is never going to be swept off his feet by mad passion, and your grand emotional overtures may not be recognized as such simply because of their scale. Affection and care, yes: helpless love, no.

As business partners you should get on very well. Virgo has the ability to make you talk, which the other signs can't do very well, and you can help him develop a feel for things which is intuitive rather than analytical. The strength of the one is the weakness of the other, and there is a genuine desire to help each other along. Both of you work hard and long when necessary, though you are both prone to overwork unless reminded that you sometimes need a holiday. You are both 'collecting' signs, and have a tendency to think that working hard solves problems, which is not always true.

As marriage partners you would be very well suited, since you can both understand and be sympathetic to the other's approach to life. Remember to look outwards and upwards from time to time, though.

Cancer–Libra
This is an easy relationship to start. The pair of you get along

passably well on the surface, and your opening behaviour, the sort you use to form an acquaintance with anybody new, suits the Libran well enough. As the relationship deepens you will see fundamental differences between you at the same time as you see how much you genuinely like each other; if you manage to accept those differences and work with them rather than against them you will make a very strong partnership indeed.

Librans are almost too nice to be true on the surface. They are ruled by Venus, which means that they will always see the best in somebody rather than criticize them. There is always something about you which the Libran can find to like, and this is very flattering to you. There is no trickery: Venus is looking for something to identify with and relate to, and it has to start on the outside, because that's what it meets first. Librans like liking things: they are an outgoing sign, remember, so they are not trying to gather things into themselves. When they say they like you, it is real. You find this captivating; you can hardly believe your ears.

Librans are very refined people. They like anything which is beautiful, symmetrical, pretty, pleasing, or harmonious. This is because Venus draws them away from anything which is unbalanced or inelegant, and as a result they are all natural aesthetes. Since your behaviour pattern on meeting somebody new is unfailingly polite (that is, you stick to the formula so that you are unlikely to find yourself in a strange situation, and so that the stranger won't try to penetrate your shell), the Libran finds you attractive. After all, to him anybody with such good manners and restraint must be a balanced and refined person, and he likes that.

The trouble with this relationship is that Librans are at their best on the surface; the murky waters of the emotions are too raw and unbalanced for him. To be fair, that's not really his fault, because he isn't a Water sign, he's an Air sign, and a cardinal one at that: he is therefore as determined to make his world work in Airy terms as you are in Watery ones. You are the different tides of mental energy—he is the outgoing, communicative tide, and you are the incoming, emotional one. Because you work in the same universe but in different directions, you find each other both amenable and infuriating at the same time.

Problems arise when you are in one of your low phases. You will be feeling very possessive of him, and you will try to tell him how much you need him and how much time you have spent with him in the past. Then you will discover the meaning of the famous Libran balance. Hit him on one side, and his other side comes round to hit you in return with an exactly equal force. He will remind you of all the things that you have done to annoy him, which he has not mentioned until now. He will remind you of how much he has given in to your selfishness in the past. All of this will hurt like hell, and you will be very shocked. Libra's picture in the heavens is not an animal, it's a machine—what else did you expect?

Realize that he deals with everybody equally, and that he dislikes anything which emphasizes one person's needs above another's, and you will do well. Show him your inner self, and let him like it. Offer him your care in return. Achieve a *balance*.

As lovers, you will emphasize the softer sides of your natures, and the union will have a romantic flavour to it. As marriage or business partners you will do well if you maintain the balance: forgive his occasional vagueness and lack of concentration and he will forgive your worries and fussiness over little things. He is really a very good partner for you.

Cancer-Scorpio

Here the fountain meets the lake. Scorpio is the fixed Water sign. There is a lot of you in a Scorpio, but somehow he seems to be a stronger, more powerfully developed version. You are very much in awe of Scorpios, and would dearly love to be one. You don't find them frightening, but they seem so much more effective in their dealings with people than you are, and you admire this. In fact, the relationship between you is very much one of admiration on your part.

One of the most informative ways of looking at a Scorpio and comparing him to a Cancerian is to look at the zodiacal animals. A scorpion has a hard outer shell like your crab's, and he has eight legs and a pair of claws too. In addition to all this weaponry he has a lethal sting in his tail. Like you he doesn't move from his position easily, and when in serious trouble he will sting himself rather than surrender. All of these characteristics are shown by Scorpio people: you are dealing with a creature of the same shape as yourself. Not of the same reputation, though: the biggest difference between you by far is how the world treats you, which is again just the same as the animals. The world thinks of a crab as touchy and snappy; eventually it is broken with a hammer, and the meat made into sandwiches. The world fears scorpions, and stays a respectable distance away when it finds one.

You find the Scorpio so strong and determined that you can hardly believe it. If you were so determined, you think, you would burst from the pressure. Possibly so, but not Scorpios. You take energy in and put it out again in the form of caring; your main aim is to protect—yourself mainly, but those around you too. The Scorpio is past all that. He takes energy in, and keeps it there; his main aim is to control—again mainly himself, but then those around him, and eventually everybody.

Scorpios work at a very intense level indeed. Since this is all emotional energy, you think you are familiar with it, but the sheer scale and scope of it frightens you, and you fear for your safety. That's the trouble with you, according to the Scorpio: you care for your safety, always wondering if you will get hurt. Scorpios don't care for their own safety. They know they will survive, and can take enormous risks as long as all the elements of danger are under control. Control is their motivation, and power their goal.

You will find a relationship at this level very exciting. You must not think of the risks, only of the passion. If you feel safe with them, you could find yourself sharing in their manipulations, and enjoying the sort of power you have always felt attracted towards.

From you, the Scorpio gets a reminder of the true nature of emotional energy. You generate it freely from within yourself, whereas he doesn't. You can give emotional energy out to people in the form of care and protection, knowing that there is always going to be more where that came from; your resource is infinite—after all, you are the definition of emotions, the cardinal Water sign. The Scorpio has to keep and control the emotions he has, because he feels that he has no way of making more. Your simple maternal impulses make him feel ashamed of himself; he knows he could never show that kind of devotion. You are the shy and uncertain possessor of the most powerful gift of all. The zodiac works that way, and so, of course, does life.

On all levels, this relationship is powerful and productive, good for both of you. If you can stand the pressure, you'll love the heat! When Scorpio tries to control you, you can defend yourself quite well, and in return you can protect him from having to sting himself.

Cancer-Sagittarius

This is one of the two five-signs-apart relationships you can form. Such pairings are not at all rare, but there is a lot of work to be done by the two people concerned, because in almost every possible way you are different. A lot of patience and a willingness to adapt is required for this one to work.

You are very sensitive to what people think about you, and you are easily hurt by unkind words. Within ten minutes of meeting a Sagittarian, you will feel that you have been probed, prodded, exposed, inspected, and finally beaten up and left to die by the roadside. And yet the Sagittarian is so charming with it! How does he do it, and why is he so cruel to you?

Sagittarians are insatiably curious. They have to find out all they can about everything they meet. When they meet you, you are likely to be polite but reserved, and show a genuine concern for his welfare. How interesting, he thinks. He decides to find out more. This is not cruelty, this is the Sagittarian showing you how interested he is in you. He has an alarming talent for looking right into people and seeing their inner workings as though they were transparent. He also has a facility with words, and a desire to tell you what he has seen. They have no tact. Not one molecule. It doesn't matter where you are, or who you are with;

they have to tell it as they see it, there and then. Don't even attempt to explain your embarrassment, just slip back into your shell and play with the hors d'oeuvres, for whatever else is around at the time. There is a great deal of similarity between the Sagittarian and the puppy who keeps bringing you things he has found in the garden. You don't want them, but you know that he is showing his affection. Why do you find Sagittarians so irresistible, then?

They are warm, they are open-hearted, they are free with their emotions, they are romantic, and they are always optimists. That's why. You need them to put some warmth into your world, and to show you that life isn't as hard as you make it seem. What they need in return is somebody who really does get cheered by their relentless optimism, somebody to comfort them when their schemes collapse, and somebody to look after the serious side of life for them. They know that they do have to show a sense of responsibility now and again, over such things as mortgages and taxes, but it really doesn't suit them, and they tend to shy away from it all. You can provide the home base that they need, look after the organizational side of things, and they will provide you with an exciting life in return.

You will argue over money. You are very careful with your money, and save it whenever you can because it adds to your security. Sagittarians have never understood the word 'security', and they like spending money as fast as they can. If they start to spend *your* money, there will be arguments.

If you are lovers you must try to allow for the fact that the Sagittarian is often in love with more than one person at once. You cannot expect his exclusive attention. Think of yourself as number one wife in a harem instead. Remember that he doesn't do any of this to hurt you, and indeed wouldn't hurt you for the world: he just has to keep moving, and you find that upsetting.

If you want to make a marriage out of this, you will have to be prepared to move around, and make sudden changes. It's not as hard as it sounds—a crab, like a snail, takes his house with him when he moves. You don't lose emotional ties just by changing direction, you know.

Cancer-Capricorn

As with most of the relationships formed by two people from opposite signs of the zodiac, this one is quite easy to handle, and in fact is concerned with the same thing, which you approach in different ways.

In this case, the thing you both like so much is organization, or structure. You like organized things so that you can use the strength of the organization as a shield against your enemies: Capricorns like structures so that they can use them as ladders to climb to the top.

If you remember the example of the box which was mentioned in 'The Essential Cancer' (page 28), then you can use the same motif to understand the Capricorn's motivation: you use the box as a container for your private world, and he uses the box as a platform to stand on and be noticed.

The Capricorn is concerned with material things in the same way that you are concerned with emotional things. He uses people's reactions to material things to define his world; in other words, he gets his status from status symbols. That sounds a little hollow, but a Capricorn is more than a status symbol collector; he is the one who first decides that such things are status symbols in the first place. He wants to be noticed and recognized for his achievements and is prepared to work very hard to get what he wants. He also wants that recognition to be permanent, and to him the best way of doing that is to make it physical. It means much more to him to have a silver trophy than to win the race: the elation of winning only lasts for a day or two, or until the press has forgotten about it, but the trophy stands on his sideboard for ever. He will need to invent a whole vocabulary of success in visible form, so that people are constantly reminded of his achievements, and see him as a success. Now you see why he likes status symbols. It is expected of him. If a Capricorn chooses to display some new and expensive object, it becomes a status symbol simply because it is the sort of thing a Capricorn would have.

Given the choice, Cancer would like to be a private individual, safe with his family. Given the choice, Capricorn would like to be on public display, and known for who he is. Successful Capricorns who are millionaire recluses are only that way because it draws attention to their status; in earlier societies where there were no newspapers with gossip columns, the Capricorns were the ones with the bands of armed guards who went about reminding you how powerful they were.

What attracts you to a Capricorn? Determination, mostly; that and their withdrawn exterior. When you meet one, you will perhaps think that you are looking at a similar individual to yourself, who keeps his feelings to himself. This isn't really so: Capricorns are serious and withdrawn, true, but their emotional level is so low that you wouldn't recognize it. Emotions aren't the sort of things that you build firm reputations and business empires on, so they don't give them a lot of time. Perhaps you admire his strong determination to have things his way, no matter how long it takes him to get there; perhaps you like the self-control he shows in the face of adversity; perhaps it is simply the fact that the world looks up to him. It may even be that he recognizes the importance of the rules in life, just the same as you do. In return, you can show him that a heart of stone is capable of being warmed, and that success with people is as rewarding as success with material things.

As lovers, you will be the warmer partner, which means that the union will be a cool one—if you want love rather than sex, don't choose a Capricorn.

As business partners, you will do very well. Both of you understand the way money works, and have the knack of acquiring it. The office could be a humourless place at times, though.

As a marriage, this one is very traditional, but none the worse for that. Home life will be rather formal: Capricorn is the father figure, Cancer the mother figure, and the roles will be adhered to.

Cancer-Aquarius

This is the second of the five-signs-apart pairings you can be involved in. Like the Sagittarian one, there are massive adjustments to be made by both of you if the relationship is to develop satisfactorily, and again the principal stumbling-block is the other person's unwillingness to stay in one place for too long.

Aquarius is the second sign to be governed by Saturn; this time, unlike Capricorn, the Saturn influence is itself of a lunar type (remind yourself by looking at the horseshoe diagram and reading page 24 again). This is a cool, low-key relationship. To extend the musical metaphor—rightly, since most of what an Aquarian does can be explained in musical terms—it is an off-beat relationship too, based on fascination and a certain quirky amusement rather than more regular forces like admiration or affection.

An Aquarian will leave you alone when you want it, and that makes him unique in the zodiac. You are very grateful for this, and a partner who does not swamp you with his presence has a lot of appeal for you. Sometimes it can be difficult to get him really involved when you do want him to be close to you, but you can't have everything.

Aquarians have a lot of compassion, and they do care; you recognize this and find it a sympathetic viewpoint to your own. Where you differ, though, is that they care on a general scale, whereas you care on an individual scale. Social injustice awakens the Aquarian spirit, where personal injustice excites yours. You will find it difficult to believe that they cannot scale down their concern to match yours, but it is so: they don't lack feeling, but they do lack involvement. You are intimately involved with every action you undertake, but they are not. It will take you some time to understand this devotion to the universal but distinct coolness towards the specific, because it isn't what you understand by compassion at all.

Aquarians have a fascination for the unusual; in fact the unusual is the usual for them. You are a very conventional soul, taking comfort in the familiarity of known and trusted things, but an Aquarian has to try the unknown just to see what it's like. You can't conventionalize an Aquarian—they need the unusual like you need affection. They also need large numbers of people, whereas you are happier with a small group. These two areas of difference, between the large-scale and the personal and between the unusual and the conventional, are going to crop up again and again in your relationship; you will have to make great efforts to get round them.

As friends you will get along easily, especially if you are part of a larger group. You both recognize that the other one doesn't like being pressed too hard to do anything, and you maintain a discreet distance. He likes your sensitivity and your quiet exterior. When you deepen the friendship and become lovers, you will find things more difficult. You require a personal devotion he just can't provide, and his affections lack the depth you seek. He will always be looking to change the relationship, and you to give it some sort of roots; it isn't easy.

Should you marry, you will have learnt that making emotional demands leads to trouble, and will have learnt to live with their flashes of independent behaviour. You will be keen to give your family the individual care you think they need, but he will say that you cosset them. Again, it isn't easy. Business partners? Yes, as long as you look after everything financial and he looks after everything else. It's a much better proposition than marrying him.

Cancer-Pisces
The other Water-Water partnership. Again, an animal metaphor helps you to understand how you work together. Both crabs and fishes live in the sea, surrounded by the watery element that supports them in every way. The fishes move around constantly; if they don't, they sink to the bottom. Neither of them is a threat to the other, since they don't eat each other, but occasionally the fishes get curious and come a little too close to the crab— and then they get nipped, which they don't like at all. Life between a Cancerian and a Piscean is remarkably similar.

The situation is quite similar to the Scorpio relationship, but with the roles reversed; this time the Piscean is the one lost in admiration, and you are the one who seems to have all the power and authority. Strange, isn't it? Pisces wants to be as well-protected as you are; he is horribly vulnerable to almost anything you can think of, and his complete inability to do anything assertive or decisive means that he could really do with something like your shell. You may be reserved, but you do know what you want: Pisces is pathologically shy, and has no real course of action at all.

You may think you are sensitive, but your range of sensitivity is markedly crude in comparison to the Piscean's. These people are as sensitive as a photographic plate; they catch the mere shadow of something and hold it for ever. They have a remarkable chameleon quality in that they can (and do) take on the character of their companion and his surroundings; you will find that they share your enthusiasms with you, and even dress in the same style, given long enough. Such fantastic sensitivity is a revelation to you. These people can make a whole way of life from a fleeting impression, and fashion reality from fantasy as though it were made of bricks and mortar. You wouldn't really like to be a Piscean: they have no control over what makes an impression on them next, and they cannot make emotions for themselves, only react to circumstances. No self-direction, and no structure: not your sort of thing at all.

As friends, you have coincident views most of the time, since your opinions are both shaped by similar reactions to external events. The difference is that you respond to external stimuli by deciding whether or not you need to deal with them as a threat, while the Piscean just reacts, and has to see where that gets him. You do not have his amazing flexibility, nor his adaptability, but you do have some measure of control over your life, which he doesn't. You must be careful not to defend yourself too strongly if he threatens your privacy; just a word is enough to a Piscean, and if you hurt them with your crab's claws you will do far more damage than you intended.

As lovers, you will surround yourselves with every emotional indulgence, and everything that produces a response from the senses. Romance is the keynote of this liaison rather than passion or power; roses and poetry are going to feature more frequently than sexual athletics. It could get a bit *too* dreamy for you, since you are cardinal in quality, and don't ever lose sight of the central objective. It will certainly be a luxurious experience.

As business partners, you really lack the edge required to make any sort of mark in the commercial world. The media loves Pisceans, though, so perhaps you could aim yourselves in that direction. You are best as employees rather than employers, though.

As a marriage partner, you could hardly do better. Most of the time they see things the same way as you do, and when they are being over-sensitive you can protect them as you so like to do. You can build a safe base for your family filled with love and understanding instead of tension and defensiveness. You will have to take the decisions, though: a Piscean just can't!

Part 3

Your Life

5. The Year within Each Day

You have probably wondered, in odd moments, why there are
more than twelve varieties of people. You know more than
twelve people who look completely different. You also know
more than one person with the same Sun sign as yourself who
doesn't look anything like you. You also know two people who
look quite like each other, but who are not related, and do not
have birthdays near each other, so can't be of the same Sun sign.
You will have come to the conclusion that Sun signs and
astrology don't work too well, because anyone can see that there
are more than twelve sorts of people.

You will also have wondered, as you finished reading a
newspaper or magazine horoscope, how those few sentences
manage to apply to a twelfth of the nation, and why it is that they
are sometimes very close to your true circumstances, and yet at
other times miles off. You will have come to the conclusion that
astrology isn't all that it might be, but some of it is, and that you
like it enough to buy magazines for the horoscopes, and little
books like this one.

It might be that there is some other astrological factor, or
factors, which account for all the different faces that people
have, the similarities between people of different Sun signs, and
the apparent inconsistencies in magazine horoscopes. There
are, indeed, lots of other astrological factors we could consider,
but one in particular will answer most of the inconsistencies we
have noticed so far.

It is the Ascendant, or rising sign. Once you know your Ascendant, you will see how you get your appearance, your way of working, your tastes, your preferences and dislikes, and your state of health (or not, as the case may be). It is perhaps of more use to you to consider yourself as belonging to your Ascendant sign, than your Sun sign. You have been reading the wrong newspaper horoscopes for years; you are not who you thought you were!

You are about to protest that you know when your birthday is. I'm sure you do. This system is not primarily linked to your birthday, though. It is a smaller cogwheel in the clockwork of the heavens, and we must come down one level from where we have been standing to see its movements. Since astrology is basically the large patterns of the sky made small in an individual, there are a number of 'step-down' processes where the celestial machinery adjusts itself to the smaller scale of mankind; this is one of them.

Here's the theory:

Your birthday pinpoints a particular time during the year. The Sun appears to move round the strip of sky known as the zodiac during the course of the year. In reality, of course, our planet, Earth, moves round the Sun once a year, but the great friendly feature of astrology is that it always looks at things from our point of view; so, we think we stand still, and the Sun appears to move through the zodiac. On a particular day of importance, such as your birthday, you can see which of the zodiac signs the Sun is in, pinpoint how far it has gone in its annual trip round the sky, and then say 'This day is important to me, because it is my birthday; therefore this part of the sky is important to me because the Sun is there on my special day. What are the qualities of that part of the Sun's journey through the zodiac, and what are they when related to me?' The answer is what you usually get in a horoscope book describing your Sun sign.

Fine. Now let's go down one level, and get some more detail. The Earth rotates on its own axis every day. This means that, from our point of view, we stand still and the sky goes round us once a day. Perhaps you hadn't thought of it before, but that's how the Sun appears to move up and across the sky from sunrise to sunset. It's actually us who are moving, but we see it the other way round. During any day, then, your birthday included, the whole of the sky goes past you at some time or another; but at a particular moment of importance, such as the time that you were born, you can see where the Sun is, see which way up the sky is, and say, 'This moment is important to me, because I was born at this time; therefore the layout of the sky has the same qualities as I do. What are the qualities of the sky at this time of day, and what are they when related to me?'

You can see how you are asking the same questions one level lower down. The problem is that you don't know which bit of the sky is significant. Which bit do you look at? All you can see? All that you can't (it's spherical from your point of view, and has no joins; half of it is below the horizon, remember)?

How about directly overhead? A very good try; the point in the zodiac you would arrive at is indeed significant, and is used a lot by astrologers, but there is another one which is more useful still. The eastern horizon is the point used most. Why? Because it fulfils more functions than any other point. It gives a starting point which is easily measurable, and is even visible (remember, all astrology started from observations made before mathematics or telescopes). It is also the contact point between the sky and the earth, from our point of view, and thus symbolizes the relationship between the sky and mankind on the earth. Finally, it links the smaller cycle of the day to the larger one of the year, because the Sun starts its journey on the eastern horizon each day as it rises; and, if we are concerned with a special moment, such as the time of your birth, then the start of the day, or the place that it started, at any rate, is analogous to the start of your life. Remember that you live the qualities of the moment you were born for all of your life; you are that moment made animate.

The point in the zodiac, then, which was crossing the eastern horizon at the time you were born, is called the Ascendant. If this life. Remember that you live the qualities of the moment you were born for all of your life; you are that moment made animate.

The point in the zodiac, then, which was crossing the eastern

STAR TIME (HOURS)

| 0 | 1 | 2 | 3 | 4 | 5 | 6 | 7 | 8 | 9 | 10 | 11 | 12 | 13 | 14 | 15 | 16 | 17 | 18 | 19 | 20 | 21 | 22 | 23 | 0 |

LEO

	GLASGOW	LEO (10 20)	VIRGO (10 20)	LIBRA (10 20)	SCORPIO (10 20)	SAGITTARIUS (10 20)	CAPRICORN (10 20)	AQUARIUS	PISCES	ARIES	TAURUS	GEMINI (10 20)	CANCER (10 20)
	MANCHESTER	LEO (10 20)	VIRGO (10 20)	LIBRA (10 20)	SCORPIO (10 20)	SAGITTARIUS (10 20)	CAPRICORN (10 20)	AQUARIUS	PISCES	ARIES	TAURUS	GEMINI (10 20)	CANCER (10 20)
	LONDON	LEO (10 20)	VIRGO (10 20)	LIBRA (10 20)	SCORPIO (10 20)	SAGITTARIUS (10 20)	CAPRICORN (10 20)	AQUARIUS	PISCES	ARIES	TAURUS	GEMINI (10 20)	CANCER (10 20)

CANCER

Different signs are on the horizon at different times according to where you live, as you can see. This is because of the difference in latitude. If you live in between the places given, you can make a guess from the values here. To compensate for longitude, subtract twelve minutes from your birthtime if you live in Glasgow, Liverpool or Cardiff; ten minutes for Edinburgh or Manchester, and six minutes for Leeds, Tyneside, or the West Midlands. *Add* four minutes for Norwich.

horizon at the time you were born, is called the Ascendant. If this happened to be somewhere in the middle of Gemini, then you have a Gemini Ascendant, or Gemini rising, whichever phrase you prefer. You will see that this has nothing to do with the time of year that you were born, only with the time of day.

Have a look at the diagrams on page 70, which should help explain things. If two people are born on the same day, but at different times, then the Ascendant will be different, and the Sun and all the other planets will be occupying different parts of the sky. It makes sense to assume, then, that they will be different in a number of ways. Their lives will be different, and they will look different. What they will have in common is the force of the Sun in the same sign, but it will show itself in different ways because of the difference in time and position in the sky.

How do you know which sign was rising over the eastern horizon when you were born? You will have to work it out. In the past, the calculation of the Ascendant has been the subject of much fuss and secrecy, which astrologers exploit to the full, claiming that only they can calculate such things. It does take some doing, it is true, but with a few short cuts and a calculator it need only take five minutes.

Here is the simplest routine ever devised for you to calculate your own Ascendant, provided that you know your time of birth. Pencil your answers alongside the stages as you go, so you know where you are.

1. Count forwards from 21 June to your birthday: 21 June is 1, 22 June is 2, and so on.
2. Add 273 to this. New total is: . . . .
2. Add 212 to this. New total is: . . . .
3. Divide by 365, and then
4. Multiply by 24. Answer is now: . . . .
   (Your answer by now is between 0 and 24. If it isn't, you have made a mistake somewhere. Go back and try again.)
5. Add your time of birth, in 24-hour clock time. If you were born at 3 p.m., that means 15. If you were born in Summer

Time, take one hour off. If there are some spare minutes, your calculator would probably like them in decimals, so it's 0.1 of an hour for each six minutes. 5.36 p.m. is 17.6, for example. Try to be as close as you can. New total is: . . . .

6. If your total exceeds 24, subtract 24. Your answer must now be between 0 and 24. Answer is: . . . .

7. You have now got the time of your birth not in clock time, but in sidereal, or star, time, which is what astrologers work in. Page 70 has a strip diagram with the signs of the zodiac arranged against a strip with the values 0 to 24, which are hours in star time. Look against the time you have just calculated, and you will see which sign was rising at the time you were born. For example, if your calculated answer is 10.456, then your Ascendant is about the 16th degree of Scorpio.

What Does the Ascendant Do?

Broadly speaking, the Ascendant does two things. Firstly, it gives you a handle on the sky, so that you know which way up it was at the time you entered the game, so to speak; this has great significance later on in the book, when we look at the way you handle large areas of activity in your life such as your career, finances, and ambitions. Secondly, it describes your body. If you see your Sun sign as your mentality and way of thinking, then your Ascendant sign is your body and your way of doing things. Think of your Sun sign as the true you, but the Ascendant as the vehicle you have to drive through life. It is the only one you have, so you can only do with it the things of which it is capable, and there may be times when you would like to do things in a different way, but it 'just isn't you'. What happens over your life is that your Sun sign energies become specifically adapted to express themselves to their best via your Ascendant sign, and you become an amalgam of the two. If you didn't, you would soon become very ill. As a Cancerian with, say, a Virgo Ascendant, you do things from a Cancerian motivation, but in a Virgo way, using a Virgo set of talents and abilities, and a Virgo body. The next few sections of the book explain what this means for each of the Sun/Ascendant combinations.

Some note ought to be made of the correspondence between the Ascendant and the actual condition of the body. Since the Ascendant sign represents your physical frame rather than the personality inside it, then the appearance and well-being of that frame is also determined by the Ascendant sign. In other words, if you have a Libra Ascendant, then you should look like a Libran, and you should be subject to illnesses in the parts of the body with a special affinity to that sign.

The Astrology of Illness

This is worth a book in itself, but it is quite important to say that the astrological view of illness is that the correlation between the individual and the larger universe is maintained. In other words, if you continue over a long period of time with a way of behaviour that denies the proper and necessary expression of your planetary energies, then the organ of your body which normally handles that kind of activity for your body systems will start to show the stresses to you. A simple example: Gemini looks after the lungs, which circulate air, and from which oxygen is taken all over the body. Gemini people need to circulate among a lot of people, talking and exchanging information. They act as the lungs of society, taking news and information everywhere. They need to do this to express their planetary energies, and society needs them to do this or it is not refreshed, and does not communicate. You need your lungs to do this, too. Lungs within people, Geminis within society: same job, different levels. If you keep a Gemini, or he keeps himself, through circumstance or ignorance, in a situation where he cannot talk or circulate, or where he feels that his normal status is denied, then he is likely to develop lung trouble. This need not be anything to do with a dusty atmosphere, or whether he smokes, although obviously neither of those will help; they are external irritants, and this is an internal problem caused by imbalance in the expression of the energies built into him since birth. In the sections which follow, all the observations on health are to do with how the body shows you that certain behaviour is unbalancing you and causing unnecessary stress; problems from these causes are alleviated by listening to yourself and changing your behaviour.

Your Ascendant

Aries Ascendant
If you have Aries rising, you are an uncommon individual, because Aries only rises for about fifty minutes out of the twenty-four hour day. You must have been born at around midnight, or else you have got your sums wrong somewhere.

What you are trying to do with yourself is project a Cancerian personality through an Arian vehicle. You will always be trying to do things faster than anybody else, and this can lead to hastiness and a certain degree of accident-proneness. What you see as the correct way to do things involves immediate action by the most direct method, to secure instant, and measurable, results. You feel that unless you are directly and personally responsible for doing things, then they cannot be done, not only because you believe that only you can do them properly, but because you get no satisfaction from letting anybody else do anything. Personal experience of everything is the only way you learn; reading about it, or watching it, does nothing for you.

You are likely to have headaches as a recurring problem if you push yourself too hard, and you should watch your blood pressure too. Mars, ruling Aries, is a strong and forceful planet, and it is bound to get you a little over-stressed at times. You are also likely to have problems digesting things properly. Astrologically, all illnesses apply to your external condition as well as your internal condition, so think carefully; when your head aches you are banging it too hard against a problem which cannot be overcome that way, and when you are not digesting properly, you have not understood the implications of what you have taken on. In both cases, allow time to think and consider.

Taurus Ascendant

You were born shortly after midnight if you have Taurus rising. Taureans are generally fond of food—do you celebrate your birth-time by sneaking down to the fridge for a midnight snack? You should have all the Taurean physical characteristics: quite thick-set, big around the neck and shoulders sometimes, and with large hands. You should have a broad mouth, and large eyes, which are very attractive. You should also have a good voice—not only as a singing voice, but one which is pleasant to listen to in conversation too.

The Taurean method for getting things done is to look forward to, and then enjoy, the material reward for one's efforts. It is part of Taurean thinking that if you can't touch it, buy it, own it or eat it, it isn't real and it isn't worth much. You will also be concerned to keep what is yours, not to waste your energies on what won't gain you anything or increase your possessions, and not to attempt anything which you don't think you have more than a chance of achieving.

Taureans do have taste; not only taste for food, which they love, but artistic taste, which they develop as a means of distinguishing things of value which they would then like to acquire and gain pleasure from owning. Unlike the Capricorn way of doing things, which values quality because it is valued by others, Taureans enjoy their possessions for themselves. The drawback to the Taurean approach is the lack of enterprise, and the unwillingness to try things just for the fun of it.

Taurean Ascendant people have throat and glandular problems, and all problems associated with being overweight. They can also have back and kidney problems caused as a result of an unwillingness to let things go in their external life. A lighter touch is needed in the approach to problems of possession; shedding unwanted or outworn things in a desirable process.

Gemini Ascendant

If you have a Gemini Ascendant you were born before sunrise. You should have expressive hands and a wide range of gestures which you use as you speak (ask your friends!) and you are perhaps a little taller than average, or than other members of your family. Gemini Ascendant people also have dark hair, if there is any possibility of it in their parents' colouring, and quick, penetrating eyes which flash with amusement and mischief; Gemini Ascendant women have very fine eyes indeed.

The Gemini approach to things, which you find yourself using, is one in which the idea of a thing is seen as being the most useful, and in which no time must be lost in telling it to other people so that they can contribute their own ideas and responses to the discussion. The performance of the deed is of no real importance in the Gemini view; somebody else can do that. Ideas and their development are what you like to spend time on, and finding more people to talk to, whose ideas can be matched to your own, seems to you to offer the most satisfaction.

There are two snags to the Gemini approach. The first is that there is a surface quality to it all, in which the rough outline suffices, but no time is spent in development or long-term experience. It may seem insignificant, but there is some value in seeing a project through to the end. The second snag is similar, but is concerned with time. The Gemini approach is immediate, in that it is concerned with the present or the near future. It is difficult for a Gemini Ascendant person to see farther than a few months into the future, if that; it is even more difficult for him to extend his view sideways in time to see the impact of his actions on a wider scene. Both of these things he will dismiss as unimportant.

Gemini Ascendant people suffer from chest and lung maladies, especially when they cannot communicate what they want to or need to, or when they cannot circulate socially in the way that they would like. They also have problems eliminating wastes from their bodies, through not realizing the importance of ending things as well as beginning them. In both cases, thinking and planning on a broader scale than usual, and examination of the past to help make better use of the future, is beneficial.

Cancer Ascendant

You were born at sunrise if you have both the Sun and the

Ascendant in Cancer. The Cancerian frame, through which you project your energies, may mean that you appear a little round and not so muscular as other Cancerians. Your energies are in no way diminished; in fact, you are likely to be even more determined, and be described in newspaper clichés like 'small and soft to look at, but with a will of steel'. Your face could be almost cherubic, and you could have small features in a pale complexion with grey eyes and brown hair. The key to the Cancer frame is that it is paler than usual, less well defined, and has no strong colouring. Strong noses and red hair do not come from a Cancerian Ascendant.

The Cancerian approach to things is highly personal. All general criticisms are taken personally, and all problems in any procedure for which they have responsibility is seen as a personal failing. You will be concerned to use your energies for the safe and secure establishment of things from the foundations up, so that you know that whatever you have been involved in has been done properly, and is unlikely to let you down in any way; you are concerned for your own safety and reputation. As a double Cancerian, so to speak, you are likely to be almost obsessionally cautious and correct in your approach; having two shells doesn't seem to make you twice as confident at all. The other side of this approach is that you can be a little too concerned to make sure everything is done personally, and be unwilling to entrust things to other people. Not only does this overwork you, it seems obsessive and uncooperative to others.

The Cancer Ascendant person has health problems with the maintenance of the flow of fluids in his body, and a tendency to stomach ulcers caused by worry. Cancer Ascendant women should pay special attention to their breasts, since the affinity between the sign, the Moon as ruler of all things feminine, and that particular body system means that major imbalances in the life are likely to show there first. There could also be some problems with the liver and the circulation of the legs; the answer is to think that, metaphorically, you do not have to support everybody you know: they can use their own legs to stand on, and you do not have to feed them either.

Leo Ascendant

You were born around breakfast time if you have Leo as an Ascendant sign. Leo, as the determinant of the physical characteristics, makes itself known by the lion of the sign—you can always spot the deep chest, proud and slightly pompous way of walking, and, more often than not, the hair arranged in some sort of a mane, either full or taken back off the face, and golden if possible. Leo Ascendant people have strong voices and a definite presence to them. Cancer Sun and Leo Ascendant will bring to the fore any hereditary tendency to golden colouring, so a less pale complexion, or golden hair, or even freckles, may be in evidence, as will a heavy build in the upper half of the body.

The Leonine way of doing things is to put yourself in the centre and work from the centre outwards, making sure that everybody knows where the commands are coming from. It is quite a tiring way of working; you need to put a lot of energy into it, because you are acting as the driving force for everybody else. Preferred situations for this technique are those where you already know, more or less, what's going to happen; this way you are unlikely to be thrown off balance by unexpected developments. The grand gesture belongs to the Leo method; it works best if all processes are converted into theatrical scenes, with roles acted rather than lived. Over-reaction, over-dramatization, and over-indulgence are common, but the approach is in essence kind-hearted and well-meant. Children enjoy being with Leo Ascendant people, and they enjoy having children around them. The flaws in the approach are only that little gets done in difficult circumstances where applause and appreciation are scarce commodities, and that little is attempted that is really new and innovatory.

The health problems of the Leo Ascendant person come from the heart, and also from the joints, which suffer from mobility problems. These both come from a lifetime of being at the centre of things and working for everybody's good, and from being too stiff and unwilling to try any change in position. The remedy, of course, is to be more flexible, and to allow your friends to repay the favours they owe you.

Virgo Ascendant

A mid-morning birth puts Virgo on the Ascendant. Physically, this should make you slim and rather long, especially in the body; even if you have broad shoulders you will still have a long waist. There is a neatness to the features, but nothing notable; hair is brown, but again nothing notable. The nose and chin are often well-defined, and the forehead is often both tall and broad; the voice can be a little shrill and lacks penetration.

The Virgoan Ascendant person does not have an approach to life; he has a *system*. He analyses everything and pays a lot of attention to the way in which he works. It is important to the person with Virgo rising not only to be effective, but to be efficient; you can always interest them in a new or better technique. They watch themselves work, as if from a distance, all the while wondering if they can do it better. They never mind repetition; in fact they quite enjoy it, because as they get more proficient they feel better about things. A Cancerian with a Virgo Ascendant will want to know how anything and everything works; you will not be able to take anything for granted, and will have to devote all your attention to things until you have mastered their intricacies for yourself. There is a willingness to help others, to be of service through being able to offer a superior technique, inherent in the Virgo way of doing things, which prevents Virgo rising people from being seen as cold and unfriendly. This is particularly true in the case of the Cancerian with Virgo rising. They appreciate their help being appreciated. The problems in the Virgo attitude are a tendency to go into things in more detail than is necessary, and to be too much concerned with the 'proper' way to do things.

People with a Virgo Ascendant are susceptible to intestinal problems and circulatory problems, and may be prone to poor sight. All of these are ways in which the body registers the stresses of being too concerned with digesting the minutiae of things which are meant to be passed through anyway, and by not getting enough social contact. The remedy is to lift your head from your workbench sometimes, admit that the act is sometimes more important than the manner of its performance, and not to take things too seriously.

Libra Ascendant

You were born around noon if you have Libra rising; it will give you a pleasant and approachable manner which will do a great deal to hide your anxieties and prevent people thinking anything but the best of you. This will make for great success in your chosen career, whatever it is. No matter what the job is, being born around the middle of the day guarantees public prominence whether you want it or not. You should be tallish, and graceful, as all Libra Ascendant people tend to be, have a clear complexion, and often blue eyes, set in an oval face with finely-formed features.

The Libra Ascendant person has to go through life at a fairly relaxed pace. The sign that controls his body won't let him feel rushed or anxious; if that sort of thing looks likely, then he will slow down a little until the panic's over. There is a need to see yourself reflected in the eyes of others, and so you will form a large circle of friends. You define your own opinion of yourself through their responses to you, rather than being sure what you want, and not caring what they think.

The drawback to the Libran approach is that unless you have approval from others, you are unlikely to do anything on your own initiative, or at least you find it hard to decide on a course of action. You always want to do things in the way which will cause the least bother to anyone, and to produce an acceptable overall result; sometimes this isn't definite enough, and you need to know what you do want as well as what you don't.

The Libran Ascendant makes the body susceptible to all ailments of the kidneys and of the skin; there may also be trouble in the feet. The kidney ailments are from trying to take all the problems out of life as you go along. Sometimes it's better simply to attack a few of the obstacles and knock them flat in pure rage.

Scorpio Ascendant

You were probably born at lunchtime if you have Scorpio for your Ascendant sign. It should give you a dark and powerful look, with a solid build, though not necessarily over-muscled,

Scorpio Ascendant people tend to have a very penetrating and level way of looking at others, which is often disconcerting. Any possible darkness in the colouring is usually displayed, with dark complexions and dark hair, often thick and curly, never fine.

The Scorpio Ascendant person usually does things in a controlled manner. He is not given to explosive releases of energy unless they are absolutely necessary; even then, not often. He knows, or feels (a better word, since the Scorpionic mind makes decisions as a result of knowledge gained by feeling rather than thinking), that he has plenty of energy to spare, but uses it in small and effective doses, each one suited to the requirements of the task at hand. It does not seem useful to him to put in more effort than is strictly necessary for any one activity; that extra energy could be used somewhere else. The idea that overdoing things for their own sake is sometimes fun because of the sheer exhilaration of the release of energy does not strike a responsive chord in the Scorpio body, nor even much understanding. There is, however, understanding and perception of a situation which exists at more than one level. If anything is complicated, involving many activities and many people, with much interaction and many side issues which must be considered, then the Scorpio Ascendant person sees it all and understands all of it, in its minutest detail. They feel, and understand, the responses from all of their surroundings at once, but do not necessarily feel involved with them unless they choose to make a move. When they do move, they will have the intention of transforming things, making them different to conform to their ideas of how things need to be arranged.

Scorpio Ascendant people are unable simply to possess and look after anything; they must change it and direct it their way, and this can be a disadvantage.

Scorpio illnesses are usually to do with the genital and excretory systems; problems here relate to a lifestyle in which things are thrown away when used, or sometimes rejected when there is still use in them. It may be that there is too much stress on being the founder of the new, and on organizing others; this will bring head pains, and illnesses of that order. The solution is to take on the existing situation as it is, and look after it without changing any of it.

Sagittarius Ascendant

It would have been about teatime when you were born for you to have a Sagittarius Ascendant. If you have, you should be taller than average, with a sort of sporty, leggy look to you; you should have a long face with pronounced temples (you may be balding there if you are male), a well-coloured complexion, clear eyes, and brown hair. A Grecian nose is sometimes a feature of this physique.

The Sagittarian Ascendant gives a way of working that is based on mobility and change. This particular frame can't keep still and is much more comfortable walking than standing, more comfortable lounging or leaning than sitting formally. You tend to be in a bit of a hurry; travelling takes up a lot of your time, because you enjoy it so. It is probably true to say that you enjoy the process of driving more than whatever it is that you have to do when you get there. You probably think a lot of your car, and you are likely to have one which is more than just a machine for transport—you see it as an extension, a representation even, of yourself. People will notice how outgoing and friendly you seem to be, but they will need to know you for some time before they realize that you enjoy meeting people more than almost anything else, and you dislike being with the same companions all the time. There is a constant restlessness in you; you will feel that being static is somehow unnatural, and it worries you. You are an optimist, but can also be an opportunist, in that you see no reason to stay doing one thing for a moment longer than it interests you. The inability to stay and develop a situation or give long-term commitment to anything is the biggest failing of this sign's influence.

A person with Sagittarius rising can expect to have problems with his hips and thighs, and possibly in his arterial system; this is to do with trying to leap too far at once, in all senses. You may also have liver and digestive problems, again caused by haste on a long-term scale. The remedy is to shorten your horizons and concentrate on things nearer home.

Capricorn Ascendant
The Sun was setting when you were born for you to have a Capricorn Ascendant. This sign often gives a small frame, quite compact and built to last a long time, the sort that doesn't need a lot of feeding and isn't big enough or heavy enough to break when it falls over. The face can be narrow and the features small; often the mouth points downwards at the corners, and this doesn't change even when the person smiles or laughs.

The Capricorn sees life as an ordered, dutiful struggle. There is a great deal of emphasis placed on projecting and maintaining appearances, both in the professional and the personal life; the idea of 'good reputation' is one which everybody with Capricorn rising, whatever their sun sign, recognizes at once. There is a sense of duty and commitment which the Sagittarian Ascendant simply cannot understand; here the feeling is that there are things which need doing, so you just have to set to and get them done. Capricorn Ascendant people see far forwards in time, anticipating their responsibilities for years to come, even if their Sun sign does not normally function this way; in such cases they apply themselves to one problem at a time, but can envisage a succession of such problems, one after another, going on for years.

The disadvantages of this outlook are to do with its static nature. There is often a sense of caution that borders on the paranoid, and while this is often well disguised in affluent middle-class middle age, it seems a little odd in the young. This tends to make for a critical assessment of all aspects of a new venture before embarking on it, and as a result a lot of the original impetus is lost. This makes the result less than was originally hoped in many cases, and so a cycle of disappointment and unadventurousness sets in, which is difficult to break. The Capricorn Ascendant person is often humourless, and can seem determined to remain so.

These people have trouble in their joints, and break bones

from time to time, entirely as a result of being inflexible. On a small scale this can be from landing badly in an accident because the Capricorn Ascendant keeps up appearances to the very end, refusing to believe that an accident could be happening to him: on a large scale, a refusal to move with the times can lead to the collapse of an outmoded set of values when they are swept away by progress, and this breaking up of an old structure can also cripple. They can get lung troubles, too, as a result of not taking enough fresh air, or fresh ideas. The best treatment is to look after their families rather than their reputation, and to think about the difference between stability and stagnation.

Aquarius Ascendant
Having an Aquarius Ascendant means that you were born in the late evening. This will make you chattier than you would otherwise have been, with a strong interest in verbal communication. There is a certain clarity, not to say transparency, about the Aquarian physique. It is usually tall, fair, and well shaped, almost never small or dark. There is nothing about the face which is particularly distinctive; no noticeable colouring, shape of nose, brows, or any other feature. It is an average sort of face, cleanly formed and clear.

The person with an Aquarian Ascendant wants to be independent. Not violently so, not the sort of independence that fights its way out of wherever it feels it's been put, just different from everybody else. Aquarius gives your body the ability to do things in ways perhaps not done before; you can discover new techniques and practices for yourself, and don't need to stay in the ways you were taught. There is a willingness to branch out, to try new things; not a Scorpionic wish to make things happen the way you want, but an amused curiosity which would just like to see if things are any better done a different way. There is no need for you to convince the world that your way is best: it only needs to suit you.

Of course, an Aquarian needs to measure his difference against others, and therefore you feel better when you have a few friends around you to bounce ideas off, as well as showing them how you're doing things in a slightly different way. You function best in groups, and feel physically at ease when you're not the only person in the room. You are not necessarily the leader of the group; just a group member. Group leaders put their energy into the group, and you draw strength and support from it, so you are unlikely to be the leader, though paradoxically all groups work better for having you in them.

A handicap arising from an Aquarian Ascendant is that you are unlikely to really feel passionately involved with anything, and this may mean that unless you have support from your friends and colleagues you will be unable to muster the determination necessary to overcome really sizeable obstacles in your chosen career.

You are likely to suffer from diseases of the circulation and in your lower legs and ankles; these may reflect a life where too much time is spent trying to be independent, and not enough support is sought from others. You may also get stomach disorders and colds because you are not generating enough heat: get more involved in things and angrier about them!

Pisces Ascendant
You were born towards midnight if you have Pisces rising. Like Aries rising, Pisces is only possible as an Ascendant for about fifty minutes, so there aren't many of you around. Pisces Ascendant people are on the small side, with a tendency to be a bit pale and fleshy. They are not very well coordinated and so walk rather clumsily, despite the fact that their feet are often large. They have large, expressive, but rather sleepy-looking eyes.

As a Cancerian with Pisces rising, you will prefer to let things come to you than go out and look for them. You will have a very secure and private home, which functions as both a retreat and an escape for you. Although you enjoy being presented with a variety of possible actions, you feel that all of them are a little risky, and you would really prefer to stay as you are. The slightest thought of doing anything decisive or assertive has you looking around for an escape route at once. Only when backed into a corner will you make a positive move, and that is merely to get you out of the corner so that you can return to a state of indecisiveness again. You are very protective of yourself, more so than the other Cancerians; their instincts are to protect their loved ones, but yours are simple self-preservation—in a non-violent way if possible.

The major problem with a Pisces Ascendant is this inability to be active rather than reactive; you would rather be reacting to outside influences than generating your own movements from within yourself.

A Piscean Ascendant gives problems with the feet and the lymphatic system; this has connections with the way you move in response to external pressures, and how you deal with things which invade your system from outside. You may also suffer from faint-heartedness—literally as well as metaphorically. The remedy is to be more definite and less influenced by opinions other than your own.

6. Three Crosses: Areas of Life that Affect Each Other

If you have already determined your Ascendant sign from page 71, and you have read 'The Meaning of the Zodiac' on page 11, you can apply that knowledge to every area of your life with revealing results. Instead of just looking at yourself, you can see how things like your career and your finances work from the unique point of view of your birth moment.

You will remember how the Ascendant defined which way up the sky was. Once you have it the right way up, then you can divide it into sectors for different areas of life, and see which zodiac signs occupy them. After that, you can interpret each sector of sky in the light of what you know about the zodiac sign which fell in it at the time that you were born.

Below there is a circular diagram of the sky, with the horizon splitting it across the middle. This is the way real horoscopes are usually drawn. In the outer circle, in the space indicated, write the name of your Ascendant sign, not your Sun sign (unless they are the same, of course. If you don't know your time of birth, and so can't work out an Ascendant, use your Sun sign). Make it overlap sectors 12 and 1, so that the degree of your Ascendant within that sign is on the eastern horizon. Now fill in the rest of the zodiac around the circle in sequence, one across each sector boundary. If you've forgotten the sequence, look at the diagram on page 16. When you've done that, draw a symbol for the Sun (☉—a circle with a point at its centre) in one of the sectors which has your Sun sign at its edge. Think about how far through the sign your Sun is; make sure that you have put it in the right sector. Whichever sector this is will be very important to you;

having the Sun there gives a bias to the whole chart, like the weight on one side of a locomotive wheel. You will feel that the activities of that sector (or house, as they are usually called) are most in keeping with your character, and you feel comfortable doing that sort of thing.

Make sure you have got your sums right. As a Cancerian born in the late afternoon, you might well have Sagittarius rising, and the Sun in the eighth house, for example.

Now is the time to examine the twelve numbered sections of your own sky, and see what there is to be found.

Angular Houses: 1, 4, 7, 10

These are the houses closest to the horizon and the vertical, reading round in zodiacal sequence. The first house is concerned with you yourself as a physical entity, your appearance, and your health. Most of this has been dealt with in the section on

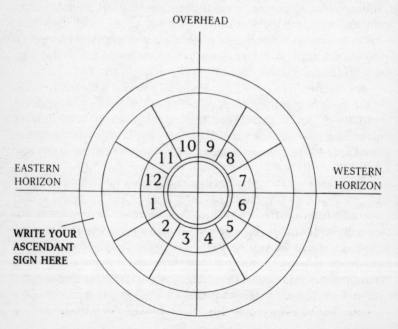

Ascendants. If you have the Sun here, it simply doubles the impact of your Sun sign energies.

Opposite to you is the seventh house, which concerns itself with everybody who is not you. Partners in a business sense, husbands, wives, enemies you are actually aware of (and who therefore stand opposed to you in plain sight) and any other unclassified strangers all belong in the seventh house. You see their motivation as being of the opposite sign to your Ascendant sign, as being something you are not. If you have Capricorn rising, you see them as behaving, and needing to be treated, which is perhaps more accurate, in a Cancerian manner. This is how you approach seventh-house things. Use the keywords from 'The Meaning of the Zodiac' (p. 17) to remind yourself what this is. If you have the Sun in the seventh house you are your own best partner: you may marry late in life, or not at all. Perhaps your marriage will be unsuccessful. It is not a failure; it is simply that you are to a very great extent self-supporting, and have neither the ability nor the need to share yourself completely with another.

The whole business of the first and the seventh is to do with 'me and not-me'. For the personal energies of this relationship to be shown in tangible form, it is necessary to look at the pair of houses whose axis most squarely crosses the first/seventh axis. This is the fourth/tenth. The tenth is your received status in the world, and is the actual answer to the question 'What do you take me for?' No matter what you do, the world will find it best to see you as doing the sort of thing shown by the sign at the start of the tenth house. Eventually, you will start to pursue that kind of activity anyway, because in doing so you get more appreciation and reward from the rest of society.

Your efforts in dealing with others, which is a first/seventh thing, have their result in the tenth, and their origins in the fourth. Expect to find clues there to your family, your home, the beliefs you hold most dear, and the eventual conclusion to your life (not your death, which is a different matter). If you have the Sun in the tenth, you will achieve some measure of prominence or fame; if your Sun is in the fourth, you will do well in property, and your family will be of greater importance to you than is usual.

There is, of course, some give and take between the paired houses. Giving more time to yourself in the first house means that you are denying attention to the seventh, your partner; the reverse also applies. Giving a lot of attention to your career, in the tenth house, stops you from spending quite so much time as you might like with your family or at home. Spending too much time at home means that you are out of the public eye. There is only so much time in a day; what you give to one must be denied to the other.

This cross of four houses defines most people's lives: self, partner, home, and career. An over-emphasis on any of these is to the detriment of the other three, and all the arms of the cross feel and react to any event affecting any single member.

If these four houses have cardinal signs on them in your chart, then you are very much the sort of person who feels that he is in control of his own life, and that it is his duty to shape it into something new, personal, and original. You feel that by making decisive moves with your own circumstances you can actually change the way your life unfolds, and enjoy steering it the way you want it to go.

If these four houses have fixed signs on them in your chart, then you are the sort of person who sees the essential shape of your life as being one of looking after what you were given, continuing in the tradition, and ending up with a profit at the end of it all. Like a farmer, you see yourself as a tenant of the land you inherited, with a responsibility to hand it on in at least as good a condition as it was when you took it over. You are likely to see the main goal in all life's ups and downs as the maintenance of stability and enrichment of what you possess.

If these four houses have mutable signs on them in your chart, then you are much more willing to change yourself to suit circumstances than the other two. Rather than seeing yourself as the captain of your ship, or the trustee of the family firm, you see yourself as free to adapt to challenges as they arise, and if necessary to make fundamental changes in your life, home and career to suit the needs of the moment. You are the sort to welcome change and novelty, and you don't expect to have anything to show for it at the end of the day except experience. There is a strong sense of service in the mutable signs, and if you spend your life working for the welfare of others, then they will have something to show for it while you will not. Not in physical terms, anyway; you will have had your reward by seeing your own energies transformed into their success.

The Succedent Houses: 2, 5, 8, 11

These houses are called succedent because they succeed, or follow on from, the previous four. Where the angular houses define the framework of the life, the succedent ones give substance, and help develop it to its fullest and richest extent, in exactly the same way as fixed signs show the development and maintenance of the elemental energies defined by the cardinal signs.

The second house and the eighth define your resources; how much you have to play with, so to speak. The fifth and eleventh show what you do with it, and how much you achieve. Your immediate environment is the business of the second house. Your tastes in furniture and clothes are here (all part of your immediate environment, if you think about it) as well as your immediate resources, food and cash. Food is a resource because without it you are short of energy, and cash is a resource for obvious reasons. If you have the Sun here you are likely to be fond of spending money, and fond of eating too! You are likely to place value on things that you can buy or possess, and judge your success by your bank balance.

Opposed to it, and therefore dealing with the opposite viewpoint, is the eighth house, where you will find stored money. Savings, bank accounts, mortgages, and all kinds of non-immediate money come under this house. So do major and irreversible changes in your life, because they are the larger environment rather than the immediate one. Surgical operations and death are both in the eighth, because you are not the same person afterwards, and that is an irreversible change. If you have the Sun in the eighth you are likely to be very careful with yourself, and not the sort to expose yourself to any risk; you are also not likely to be short of a few thousand when life gets tight, because eighth house people always have some extra resource tucked away somewhere. You are also likely to benefit from legacies, which are another form of long-term wealth.

To turn all this money into some form of visible wealth you must obviously do something with it, and all forms of self-expression and ambition are found in the fifth and the eleventh houses. The fifth is where you have fun, basically; all that you like to do, all that amuses you, all your hobbies are found there, and a look at the zodiac sign falling in that house in your chart will show you what it is that you like so much. Your children are a fifth-house phenomenon, too; they are an expression of yourself made physical, made from the substance of your body and existence, and given their own. If you have the Sun in the fifth house you are likely to be of a generally happy disposition, confident that life is there to be enjoyed, and sure that something good will turn up.

The eleventh house, in contrast, is not so much what you like doing as what you would like to be doing: it deals with hopes, wishes, and ambitions. It also deals with friends and all social gatherings, because in a similar manner to the first/seventh axis, anybody who is 'not-you' and enjoying themselves must be opposed to you enjoying yourself in the fifth house. If you have the Sun in the eleventh house, you are at your best in a group. You would do well in large organizations, possibly political ones, and will find that you can organize well. You have well-defined ambitions, and know how to realize them, using other people as supporters of your cause.

The oppositions in this cross work just as effectively as the previous set did: cash is either used or stored, and to convert it from one to the other diminishes the first. Similarly, time spent enjoying yourself does nothing for your ambitions and aims, nor does it help you maintain relationships with all the groups of people you know; there again, all work and no play . . .

If you have cardinal signs on these four houses in your chart, then you think that using all the resources available to you at any one time is important. Although what you do isn't necessarily important, or even stable, you want to have something to show for it, and enjoying yourself as you go along is important to you. To you, money is for spending, and how your friends see you is possibly more important to you than how you see yourself.

Fixed signs on these four houses will make you reticent, and careful of how you express yourself. You are possibly too busy with the important things of life as you see them, such as your career and long-term prospects, to give much attention to the way you live. You feel it is important to have things of quality, because you have a long-term view of life, and you feel secure when you have some money in the bank, but you don't enjoy your possessions and friends for your own sake. You have them because you feel that you should, not because they are reason enough in themselves.

Mutable signs on these four houses show a flexible attitude to the use of a resource, possibly because the angular houses show that you already have plenty of it, and it is your duty to use it well. You don't mind spending time and money on projects which to you are necessary, and which will have a measurable end result. You see that you need to spend time and effort to bring projects into a completed reality, and you are willing to do that as long as the final product is yours and worth having. You are likely to change your style of living quite frequently during your life, and there may be ambitions which, when fulfilled, fade from your life completely.

The Cadent Houses: 3, 6, 9, 12

The final four houses are called cadent either because they fall away from the angles (horizon and vertical axes), or because they fall towards them, giving their energy towards the formation of the next phase in their existence. Either way, affairs in these

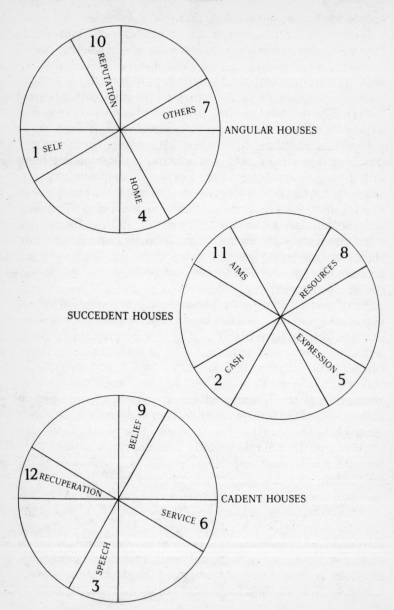

ANGULAR HOUSES

SUCCEDENT HOUSES

CADENT HOUSES

houses are nothing like as firm and active as those in the other two sets of four. It may be useful to think of them as being given to mental rather than physical or material activities.

The third and ninth houses are given to thought and speech, with the ninth specializing in incoming thoughts, such as reading, learning and belief (religions of all kinds are ninth-house things), while the third limits itself to speaking and writing, daily chat, and the sort of conversations you have every day. If you have the Sun in the third house, you will be a chatterbox. Talking is something you could do all day, and you love reading. Anything will do—papers, magazines, novels; as long as it has words in it you will like it. You will have the sort of mind that loves accumulating trivia, but you may find that serious study or hard learning is something that you cannot do.

The third house concerns itself with daily conversation, but the ninth is more withdrawn. Study is easy for a ninth-house person, but since all ideal and theoretical thought belongs here, the down-to-earth street-corner reality of the third house doesn't, and so the higher knowledge of the ninth finds no application in daily life. The third-ninth axis is the difference between practical street experience and the refined learning of a university. To give time to one must mean taking time from the other. If you have the Sun in the ninth, you are likely to have a very sure grasp of the theory of things, and could well be an instigator or director of large projects; but you are unable to actually do the things yourself. Knowledge is yours, but application is not.

How this knowledge gets applied in the production of something new is a matter of technique, and technique is the business of the sixth house. The way things get done, both for yourself and for other people's benefit, is all in the sixth. Everything you do on someone else's behalf is there, too. If you have the Sun in the sixth house, you are careful and considerate by nature, much concerned to make the best use of things and to do things in the best way possible. Pride of work and craftsman-ship are guiding words to you; any kind of sloppiness is upsetting. You look after yourself, too; health is a sixth-house thing, and the Sun in the sixth sometimes makes you something of a hypochondriac.

Opposed to the sixth, and therefore opposed to the ideas of doing things for others, mastering the proper technique, and looking after your physical health, is the twelfth house. This is concerned with withdrawing yourself from the world, being on your own, having time to think. Energy is applied to the job in hand in the sixth house, and here it is allowed to grow again without being applied to anything. Recuperation is a good word to remember. All forms of rest are twelfth-house concepts. If you have the Sun in the twelfth house you are an essentially private individual, and there will be times when you need to be on your own to think about things and recover your strength and balance. You will keep your opinions to yourself, and share very little of your emotional troubles with anyone. Yours is most definitely not a life lived out in the open.

These houses live in the shadow of the houses which follow them. Each of them is a preparation for the next phase. If your Sun is in any of these houses, your life is much more one of giving away than of accumulation. You already have the experience and the knowledge, and you will be trying to hand it on before you go, so to speak. Acquisition is something you will never manage on a permanent basis.

If these houses have Cardinal signs on them in your chart, then preparation for things to come is important to you, and you think in straight lines towards a recognized goal. You will have firm and rather simplistic views and beliefs about matters which are not usually described in such terms, such as morality and politics, and you will be used to saying things simply and with meaning. Deception and half-truths, even mild exaggeration, confuse you, because you do not think in that sort of way.

If fixed signs occupy these houses in your horoscope, your thinking is conservative, and your mind, though rich and varied in its imagination, is not truly original. You like to collect ideas from elsewhere and tell yourself that they are your own. You rely on changing circumstances to bring you variety, and your own beliefs and opinions stay fixed to anchor you in a changing world; unfortunately, this can mean a refusal to take in new ideas, shown in your behaviour as a rather appealing old-fashionedness.

Having mutable signs on these houses in your horoscope shows a flexible imagination, though often not a very practical one. Speech and ideas flow freely from you, and you are quick to adapt your ideas to suit the occasion, performing complete changes of viewpoint without effort if required. You seem to have grasped the instinctive truth that mental images and words are not real, and can be changed or erased at will; you are far less inhibited in their use than the other two groups, who regard words as something at least as heavy as cement, and nearly as difficult to dissolve. Periods in the public eye and periods of isolation are of equal value to you; you can use them each for their best purpose, and have no dislike of either. This great flexibility of mind does mean, though, that you lack seriousness of approach at times, and have a happy-go-lucky view of the future, and of things spiritual, which may lead to eventual disappointments and regrets.

Houses are important in a horoscope. The twelve sectors of the sky correspond to the twelve signs of the zodiac, the difference being that the zodiac is a product of the Sun's annual revolution, and the houses are a product (via the Ascendant) of the Earth's daily revolution. They bring the symbolism down one level from the sky to the individual, and they answer the questions which arise when people of the same Sun sign have different lives and different preferences. The house in which the Sun falls, and the qualities of the signs in the houses, show each person's approach to those areas of his life, and the one which will be the most important to him.

Part 4

Cancer Trivia

7. Tastes and Preferences

Clothes

Whatever Cancerians wear, you can be sure that the emotional and sentimental content of the garments is far more important than the colour, or whether they are currently fashionable.

Cancerians wear clothes so that they feel good, 'Good' in this context means that the wearer has happy associations with the particular garments or that they make the wearer feel a certain way. A favourite jacket, for example, may be the one which you wore all the time during a certain holiday, and so wearing it puts you in a holiday mood. Or a certain pair of shoes may make you feel like dancing, and wearing them puts you in a party mood all day. You may have a sweater or something which actually belongs to a friend of yours, but you keep it, and wear it, because it reminds you of them.

Cancererians, like the Moon, go in phases. At the beginning of a phase, you will feel that it is time for you to buy some new clothes, and so you will go out and choose some up-to-the-minute styles. Since these please you, and you feel smart in them, they soon become favourite clothes; each time you wear them you feel smart and up-to-date, even though fashions change during the time you do this. At the end of the phase, you are still very attached to your favourite clothes, although you are likely to be the only person you know still wearing that particular style. When you go browsing in the shops you find yourself looking for more clothes in the same style, because you like things with which you are familiar. After a while the shops don't seem to have any clothes like that any more, and you wonder why. When you realize what has happened, you start a new phase, and the cycle repeats. How fashionable a Cancerian looks depends on which stage of the phase they're at.

Cancerian women often go for blues and greens, though the more extroverted ones look better in white and silver, the colours of the sign. Pearlescent and iridescent finishes are lunar too, and younger Cancerians may find themselves interested in these.

Male Cancerians are conservative in dress. They are also prone to mismatching things, though this is not because they are colour-blind, or anything like that; it is because they are mindful of the sentimental association of each garment, and tend to dress in a range of pleasant thoughts without paying much attention to the overall effect!

Food and Furnishings

The Cancerian is a better host than guest, although that doesn't mean that they are ungrateful guests: far from it. As hosts, they are concerned to see that everbody has a pleasant evening, that social niceties are observed, and that nobody has to deal with anything they would choose not to. When you have them as guests, the process must be reversed.

Since Cancer is the first Water sign, it follows that the people of the sign like food that either contains a lot of liquid, or originally came in liquid, like fish. Since they are also associated with early nutrition and especially milk, then it also follows that they would like foods which are milky or creamy both in content and texture. Mousses, both sweet and savoury, will go down well, as will any form of dairy produce. Fish is the essential Water sign main course, but the Cancerian will be dismayed if there are a lot of bones to extract; it's the sort of thing that leads to mess and embarrassment, which the Cancerian will be afraid of; certainly a Cancerian host would never offer guests anything which might lead to any embarrassment in actually eating it.

Salads contain a lot of water, and a lot of salad vegetables are specifically associated with the sign. Fluid flow is vital to the Cancerian metabolism, and foods with a high water content are beneficial here. The best drink for the sign is pure water; spring water in particular has a direct connection with the sign.

The Cancerian home is exactly that. It is a home rather than a house, because it is primarily there for the Cancerian to live in and feel safe in, rather than be some sort of glossy advertisement for its owner that visitors can come and marvel at.

Because of its purpose, it is likely to be a little untidy. Cancerians put things where they would like to put them at the time, depending on their mood; when the rest of the world is looking they will mind what they are doing, but in their own homes they don't care because they don't have to.

Families are important to Cancerians, so expect the whole family to live in the whole house all of the time. Expect toys and books all over the place, and expect the furniture to be an odd mixture of the past and the present. Some of this is due to 'phases' in furniture-buying, but some of it is due to the sentimental value of the pieces themselves. Much of the furniture will be well-worn: it is important to note that it is also well-used and well-loved.

The colours will be relaxing, and usually on the pale side; nothing too strong where lunar energies are concerned. There may be one or two glass ornaments; glass is a Cancerian material, and so holds more appeal than, say, brass.

Hobbies

The pastimes and hobbies the Cancerian finds himself attracted to all have Cancerian qualities in common, which is not surprising. To be a Cancerian pastime a thing should contain as many of the following as possible: water, quietness, patience, determined strength, and sensitivity.

Sports connected with boats and the water are obviously

candidates here. Water skiing will satisfy those Cancerians with Fire signs on their Ascendants, while the less energetic sorts will enjoy fishing. Cancerian fishermen enjoy spending quiet days by the river more than actually catching anything. Wrestling is Cancerian, where boxing is Arian; it may be to do with defence rather than attack. If so, it is easy to see why chess appeals to Cancerians too.

Silversmithing is an obvious Cancerian craft, but there are less expensive ones where patience and care are the required virtues, like photography; knitting is a Cancerian craft too, with obvious links to the family and home life that are so important to the sign's way of thought.

8. Cancerian Luck

Being lucky isn't a matter of pure luck. It can be engineered. What happens when you are lucky is that a number of correspondences are made between circumstances, people, and even material items, which eventually enable planetary energies to flow quickly and effectively to act with full force in a particular way. If you are part of that chain, or your intentions lie in the same direction as the planetary flow, then you say that things are going your way, or that you are lucky. All you have to do to maximize this tendency is to make sure you are aligned to the flow of energies from the planets whenever you want things to work your way.

It is regular astrological practice to try to reinforce your own position in these things, by attracting energies which are already strongly represented in you. For a Cancer, this means the Moon, of course, and therefore any 'lucky' number, colour, or whatever for a Cancer is simply going to be one that corresponds symbolically with the attributes of the Moon.

The Moon's colours are white and silver; therefore a Cancer person's lucky colours are white and silver, because by wearing them or aligning himself to them, for example by betting on a horse whose jockey's silks are white or silver, or supporting a sporting team whose colours include white, he aligns himself to the energies of the Moon, and thereby recharges the lunar energies that are already in him.

A Cancer's preferred gemstone is a pearl, because of its colour and the reasons given above, Gemstones are seen as being able to concentrate or focus magical energies, and the colour of the stone shows its correspondence with the energies of a particular planet. Other gemstones are sometimes quoted for Cancer, such as the moonstone or some quartzes, but in most cases the colour is the key.

Because Cancer is the fourth sign, your lucky number is 4; all combinations of numbers which add up to 4 by reduction work the same way, so you have a range to choose from. Reducing a number is done by adding its digits until you can go no further. As an example, take 697, $6 + 9 + 7 = 22$, and then $2 + 2 = 4$. There you are—697 is a lucky number for you, so to buy a car with those digits in its registration plate would make it a car which, while you had it, you were very fond of, and which served you well.

The Moon has its own number, which is 9. The same rules apply as they did with 4. The Moon also has its own day, Monday (Moon Day, yes? Or lundi in French, which is the Lunar Day), and Cancer has both a time with which it is associated (midnight) and a direction (the North). If you have something important to do, and you manage to put it into action on Monday 9 April (month number 4, remember), then you will have made sure that you will get the result best suited to you, by aligning yourself to your own planet and helping its energies flow through you and your activity unimpeded.

The Moon also has a metal associated with it, and in the Middle Ages people wore jewellery made of their planetary metals for luck, or self-alignment and emphasis, whichever way you want to describe it. In the case of Cancer and the Moon, that metal is silver. You are lucky—some of the planetary metals don't look very attractive made up into jewellery, but there is an almost unlimited range of beautiful items in silver for you to choose from.

There are plants and herbs for each planet, and foods too. Among the edible plants are cabbage, lettuce, and onions. Mushrooms are lunar, too.

There is almost no end to the list of correspondences between the planets and everyday items, and many more can be made if you have a good imagination. They are lucky for Cancerians if you know what makes them so, and if you believe them to be so; the essence of the process lies in linking yourself and the object of your intent with some identifiable token of your own planet, such as its colour or number, and strengthening yourself thereby. The stronger you are, then the more frequently you will be able to achieve the result you want—and that's all that luck is, isn't it?

A Final Word

By the time you reach here, you will have learnt a great deal more about yourself. At least, I hope you have.

You will probably have noticed that I appear to have contradicted myself in some parts of the book, and repeated myself in others, and there are reasons for this. It is quite likely that I have said that your Sun position makes you one way, while your Ascendant makes you the opposite. There is nothing strange about this; nobody is consistent, the same the whole way through—everybody has contradictory sides to their character, and knowing some more about your Sun sign and your Ascendant will help you to label and define those contradictory elements. It won't do anything about dealing with them, though—that's your job, and always has been. The only person who can live your horoscope is you. Astrology won't make your problems disappear, and it never has been able to; it simply defines the problems more clearly, and enables you to look for answers.

Where I have repeated myself it is either to make the point for the benefit of the person who is only going to read that section of the book, or because you have a double helping of the energy of your sign, as in the instance of the Sun and Ascendant in the same sign.

I hope you found the relationships section useful; you may well find that the Sun-to-Ascendant comparison is just as useful in showing you how you fit in with your partner as the usual Sun-to-Sun practice.

Where do you go from here? If you want to learn more about astrology, and see how all of the planets fit into the picture of the sky as it was at your birth, then you must either consult an astrologer or learn how to do it for yourself. There is quite a lot of astrology around these days; evening classes are not too hard to find and there are groups of enthusiasts up and down the country. There are also plenty of books which will show you how to draw up and interpret your own horoscope.

One thing about doing it yourself, which is an annoyance unless you are aware of it in advance: to calculate your horoscope properly you will need to know where the planets were in the sky when you were born, and you usually have to buy this data separately in a book called an ephemeris. The reason that astrology books don't have this data in them is that to include enough for everybody who is likely to buy the book would make the book as big as a phone directory, and look like a giant book of log tables, which is a bit off-putting. You can buy ephemerides (the plural) for any single year, such as the one of your birth. You can also buy omnibus versions for the whole century.

So, you will need two books, not one: an ephemeris, and a book to help you draw up and interpret your horoscope. It's much less annoying when you *know* you're going to need two books.

After that, there are lots of books on the more advanced techniques in the Astrology Handbook series, also from the Aquarian Press. Good though the books are, there is no substitute for being taught by an astrologer, and no substitute at all for practice. What we are trying to do here is provide a vocabulary of symbols taken from the sky so that you and your imagination can make sense of the world you live in; the essential element is your imagination, and you provide that.

Astrology works perfectly well at Sun sign level, and it works perfectly well at deeper levels as well; you can do it with what you want. I hope that, whatever you do with it, it is both instructive and satisfying to you—and fun, too.

SUNS AND LOVERS

The Astrology of Sexual Relationships

Penny Thornton. It doesn't seem to matter how experienced – or inexperienced – you are, when it comes to love and romance there just *isn't* a fool proof formula. . . but this book does its best to provide one! THE definitive astrological guide to sexual relationships, this book is based upon the accumulated wisdom, and observations of centuries of dedicated astrologers. Reveals:

- In-depth analysis of astrological types
- Male and female profiles for each star sign
- Zodiacal attitudes to intimate relationships
- Most compatible – and incompatible – partners

Each general star sign analysis is concluded with amazingly frank reflections, often based upon personal interviews, with many famous personalities including: Bob Champion; Suzi Quatro; Colin Wilson; Jeremy Irons; HRH The Princess Anne; HRH The Duke of York; Martin Shaw; Barbara Cartland; Twiggy and many more. Written in an easy-to-read style, and packed with illuminating and fascinating tit-bits, this book is compulsive reading for anyone likely to have *any sort* of encounter with the opposite sex!

HOW TO ASTRO-ANALYSE YOURSELF AND OTHERS.

Mary Coleman. Easy to follow, step-by-step instructions on the art of astro-analysis a blend of traditional astrology and modern psychology that provides practical solutions to the conundrums of life, love and sex.

- Discover why you do the things you do.
- Plan your life instead of just 'letting it happen'.
- Make the most of yourself and your relationships.

Master the technique of astro-anaysis and discover a more confident 'you' emerging, and the path to a happier, more satisying future opening out before you. The day you read this book could be the first day of the rest of your life.

THE ASTROLOGY WORKBOOK

This book is YOUR introduction to FUN, FORTUNE and FASCINATION

Cordelia Mansall, in clear and easy-to-understand language, demystifies the ancient science of astrology and shows how YOU can profit from this exact, and increasingly respected, wisdom.

Discover

- When to expect your 'vitality surges'
- The crisis ages of your life
- Your hidden talents
- The latent potentialities of your children

The whole of our lives are shaped by cosmic forces. Astrology is the study of these forces and their effects upon our lives *both now and in the future*. The author shows how it can be used to bring a deeper understanding to the problems encountered in personal relationships, indicate the most favourable times for major life-style changes and present an important balance between science and spirituality. *Discover your place in the overall scheme of the universe with* THE ASTROLOGY WORKBOOK by **Cordelia Mansall D. F. Astrol. S.**